Crossway Bible Guide

Series editors: Ian Coffey (NT), Stephen Gaukroger (OT)
New Testament editor: Stephen Motyer

Titles in this series

Exodus, Stephen Dray
Leviticus, Derek Tidball
Joshua, Charles Price
Ezra and Nehemiah, Dave Cave
Psalms 1 – 72, Alan Palmer
Psalms 73 – 150, Alan Palmer and Debra Reid
Isaiah, Philip Hacking
Six minor prophets, Michael Wilcock
Haggai, Zechariah and Malachi, John James
Matthew's Gospel, Stephen Dray
Mark's Gospel, David Hewitt
Luke's Gospel, Simon Jones
John's Gospel, Ian Barclay
Acts, Stephen Gaukroger
1 Corinthians, Robin Dowling and Stephen Dray
2 Corinthians, Jonatham Lamb
Ephesians, Steve Motyer
Philippians, Ian Coffey
1 and 2 Thessalonians, Alec Motyer and Steve Motyer
Timothy and Titus, Michael Griffiths
James, David Field
1 Peter, Andrew Whitman

The Bible with Pleasure, Steve Motyer
Housegroups: The Leaders' Survival Guide, Ian Coffey and
    Stephen Gaukroger (eds.)

1 and 2 Thessalonians:
Crossway Bible Guide

Alec Motyer (1 Thessalonians)
and Steve Motyer (2 Thessalonians)

Crossway Books Leicester

CROSSWAY BOOKS
38 De Montfort Street, Leicester LE1 7GP, England

First published 1999

British Library Cataloguing in Publication Data
A catalogue record for this book is available from the British Library.

ISBN 1–85684–191–X

Set in Palatino
Typeset in Great Britain
Printed in Great Britain by Caledonian International Book Manufacturing Ltd, Glasgow

CONTENTS

Welcome!   9
How to use this Bible Guide   10
    How to tackle personal Bible study   10
    How to tackle your group Bible study   11
    How to tackle the letters to the Thessalonians   14
Finding your way round this book   16

Stop and look: what is 1 Thessalonians all about?   18
    Hello to God's transplanted people! 1:1   20
    Mission Thessalonica: how to plant a church   21

1 The basic Christian life – 1 Thessalonians 1:2–10   23
Stop and look: be a square – or a chair   24
    Delivering the goods 1:2–3   25
    Great and lovely secrets 1:4–6   27
    God's choice and ours   28
    Mimics and mouths 1:6–8   30
    Focus on the Bible   32
    Happy ever after! 1:9–10   33

**2 Commitment to the gospel, to holiness
and to people – 1 Thessalonians 2:1–16**   35
Stop and look: more 'saying and showing'   36
    The trustee 2:1–4   37
    Bible translations   39
    Concordances   39
    Tender loving care 2:5–9   40
    Apostles   43
    To encourage, to comfort and to teach 2:10–12   44
    The big issue 2:13–16   47
    Paul and the Jews   50

3 Paul's love for the Thessalonians –
   1 Thessalonians 2:17 – 4:8   51
Stop and look: the world, the flesh and the devil   52
   Your enemy the devil 2:17–20   54
   In the arena 3:1–5   56
   Winning through 3:6–10   59
   What to pray for 3:11–13   62
      Bible prayers   66
      Holiness   67
   God's holy will 4:1–8   68
   Avoid sexual immorality 4:3b–8   71
      Marriage and sex   73

4 Christian responsibilities –
   1 Thessalonians 4:9 – 5:11   77
Stop and look: caring for each other   78
   Loving one another 4:9–12   79
   What about those who have died? 4:13–15   83
   Listening for the trumpet 4:16–18   87
   Waiting for the day 5:1–3   91
   We are not in darkness 5:4–8   94
   What an assurance! 5:9–11   97

5 Ready for Christ's coming –
   1 Thessalonians 5:12–28   101
Stop and look: working for the day   102
   Encouraging one another 5:12–15   103
   The joyful will of God 5:16–18   107
   Available powers 5:19–22   109
      Prophets   113
   Paul's prayer 5:23–24   116
   Goodbye! 5:25–28   118

Stop and look: what is 2 Thessalonians all about?   121

6 The shape of the Christian life –
   2 Thessalonians 1:1–12   125
   Hello and thanks 1:1–4   126
   When will the mess get sorted? 1:5–10   129

    Eternal destruction?   132
    Class 1 priorities 1:11–12   134

7 The 'rebellion' and the coming of Jesus –
  2 Thessalonians 2:1–12   139
Stop and look: what is happening in 2:1–12?   140
    Jesus *is* coming again 2:1–3a   142
    But first ... the coming of
        'the lawless one' 2:3b–12   145
        The end of the temple?   148
    And also ... the 'rebellion' and
        the 'restrainer' 2:3b–12   150
    And then ... the coming of Jesus
        in splendour 2:3b–12   153
        Is the 'man of lawlessness' the same
        as the antichrist?   156
        Does God deceive people?   158

8 Belonging to Jesus in the meantime –
  2 Thessalonians 2:13 – 3:5   161
Stop and look: what is happening in 2:13 – 3:5?   162
    Being 'firstfruits' for him 2:13–14   163
        'From the beginning' or 'as firstfruits'?   166
    Standing for him 2:15–17   168
    Praying harvesters for him 3:1–2   171
    Facing danger for him 3:3–5   174
    Patience   177

9 Business as usual? – 2 Thessalonians 3:6–18   179
Stop and look: what is happening in 3:6–18?   180
    Having the right role model 3:6–9   182
    Working and eating 3:10–12   185
    Living in peace with each other 3:13–18   188

For further reading   192

**To
Roy and Vera Lucas,
and to
Andy and Kathy Coomar,
a very dear brother,
and one of Thessalonica's most special daughters**

Welcome!

These days, meeting together to study the Bible in groups appears to be a booming leisure-time activity in many parts of the world. In the United Kingdom alone, it is estimated that over one million people each week meet in home Bible-study groups.

This series has been designed to help such groups and, in particular, those who lead them. These Bible guides are also very suitable for individual study, and may help hard-pressed preachers, teachers and students too (see 'How to use this Bible Guide').

We have therefore enlisted authors who are in the business of teaching the Bible to others and are doing it well. They have kept in their sights two clear aims:

1. To explain and apply the message of the Bible in non-technical language.
2. To encourage discussion, prayer and action on what the Bible teaches.

All of us engaged in the project believe that the Bible is the Word of God – given to us in order that people might discover him and his purposes for our lives. We believe that the sixty-six books which go to make up the Bible, although written by different people, in different places, at different times, through different circumstances, have a single unifying theme: that theme is Salvation. This means free forgiveness and the removal of all our guilt, it means the gift of eternal life, and it means the wholeness of purpose and joy which God has designed us to experience here and now, all of this being made possible through the Lord Jesus Christ.

How to use this Bible Guide

These guides have been prepared both for personal study and for the leaders and members of small groups. More information about group study follows on the next few pages.

You can use this book very profitably as a personal study guide. The short studies are ideal for daily reading: the first of the questions provided is usually aimed to help you with personal reflection (see 'How to tackle personal Bible study'). If you prefer to settle down to a longer period of study, you can use groups of three to five studies, and thus get a better overview of a longer Bible passage. In either case, using the Bible Guide will help you to be disciplined about regular study, a habit that countless Christians have found greatly beneficial. (See also 'How to tackle the letters to the Thessalonians' for methods of selecting studies if you do not intend to use them all.)

Yet a third use for these Bible Guides is as a quarry for ideas for the busy Bible teacher, providing outlines and application for those giving talks or sermons or teaching children. You will need more than this book can offer, of course, but the way the Bible text is broken down, comments offered and questions raised may well suggest directions to follow.

How to tackle personal Bible study

We have already suggested that you might use this book as a personal study guide. Now for some more detail.

One of the best methods of Bible study is to read the text through carefully several times, possibly using different versions or translations. Having reflected on the material, it is a good discipline to write down your own thoughts before doing anything else. At this stage it can be useful to consult another background book. See 'Resources' on page 12 and 'For further reading' on page 192. If you are using this book as your main study resource, then read through the relevant sections carefully, turning up the Bible references that are mentioned. The questions at the end of each chapter are specifically designed to help you to apply the passage to your own situation. You may find it helpful to write your answers to the questions in your notes.

It is a good habit to conclude with prayer, bringing before God the things you have learned.

If this kind of in-depth study is too demanding for you and you have only a short time at your disposal, read the Bible passage, read the comments in the Bible Guide, think round one of the questions and commit what you have learned to God in a brief prayer. This would take about fifteen minutes without rushing it.

How to tackle your group Bible study

1. Getting help

If you are new to leading groups, you will obviously want to get all the help you can from ministers and experienced friends. Books are also extremely helpful and we strongly recommend a book prepared by the editors of this series of Bible Guides: *Housegroups: The Leaders' Survival Guide*, edited by Ian Coffey and Stephen Gaukroger (Crossway Books, 1996). This book looks at the whole range of different types of group, asking what is the point of it all, what makes a good leader, how to tackle your meeting, how to help the members, how to study, pray, share and worship, and plenty of other pointers, tips and guidelines.

This book is a 'must' for all leaders of small groups. It is written by a team of people widely experienced in this area. It is available at your local Christian bookshop. If you have difficulty in obtaining a copy write to Crossway Books, Norton Street, Nottingham NG7 3HR, UK.

2. Planning a programme with your Bible Guide

This guide is a commentary on God's Word, written to help a group of people to get the most out of their studies. Although it is never ideal to chop up Scripture into small pieces, which the authors never intended, huge chunks are indigestible and we have tried to provide a diet of bite-sized mouthfuls.

The book is divided into major parts, each with a title indicated by a part-title page with a large number. If you want to get an overview of the Bible book in a series of meetings you will need to select appropriate studies for each meeting. Read them yourself first and prepare a short summary of the studies you are tackling for your group. Ideally you could write it on a sheet of A5 paper and hand a copy to each member. Then choose one study from the part you are dealing with as a basis for your meeting. Do not attempt to pack more than one study into one meeting but choose the crucial one, the study which best crystallizes the message. There are examples in 'How to tackle the letters to the Thessalonians' below.

If you do not intend to cover the whole two Bible books, choose a series of studies to suit the number of meetings you have available. Each part of the commentary is divided into a few (usually 3–5) studies. It is a good idea to use consecutive studies, not to dodge about. You will then build up a detailed picture of one section of Scripture. Alternative examples of programmes of study for these two books are given in 'How to tackle the letters to the Thessalonians'.

3. Resources

You will find any or all of these books of great value in providing background to your Bible knowledge. Put some of them on your Christmas list and build up your library.

New Bible Dictionary or *New Concise Bible Dictionary* (IVP)
New Bible Atlas (IVP)
New Bible Commentary (21st Century edition) (IVP)
Handbook of Life in Bible Times by John Thompson (IVP)

The Bible User's Manual (IVP)
The Lion Handbook to the Bible (Lion Publishing)
The Message of the Bible (Lion Publishing)
NIV *Study Bible* (Hodder & Stoughton)
The Bible with Pleasure by Steve Motyer (Crossway Books)

˙ The relevant volume in the IVP Tyndale Commentary series will give you reliable and detailed help with any knotty points you may encounter.

4. Preparing to lead

Reading, discussing with friends, studying, praying, reflecting on life ... preparation can be endless. But do not be daunted by that. If you wait to become the perfect leader you will never start at all. The really vital elements in preparation are:

▶ prayer (not only in words but an attitude of dependence on God: 'Lord, I can't manage this on my own')

▶ familiarity with the study passage (careful reading of the text, the Bible Guide study and any other resource books that throw light on it) and

▶ a clear idea of where you hope to get in the meeting (notes on your introduction, perhaps, recap what was covered at the last meeting, and what direction you hope the questions will take you in – don't force the group to give your answers).

Here is a short checklist for the busy group leader:

Have I prayed about the meeting?
Have I decided exactly what I want to achieve through the meeting?
Have I prepared the material?
Am I clear about the questions that will encourage positive group discussion?
Am I gently encouraging silent members?

Am I, again gently, quietening the chatterers?

Am I willing to admit ignorance?

Am I willing to listen to what the group members say and to value their contributions?

Am I ready not to be dogmatic, not imposing my ideas on the group?

Have I planned how to involve the members in discovering for themselves?

Have I developed several 'prayer points' that will help focus the group?

Are we applying Scripture to our experience of real life or only using it as a peg to hang our opinions on?

Are we finding resources for action and change or just having a nice talk?

Are we all enjoying the experience together?

How to tackle the letters to the Thessalonians

Now let's assume that you're planning an eight-week course of studies (you will have to make the adjustments if you have more or fewer meetings). Where do you begin? This is entirely up to you and your group, of course, but, to get you started, here are a few possible routes you might take.

1. Basic Christian living

There are eight studies covering 1 Thessalonians 1:1 – 2:16, setting out the major themes of the basic Christian life and commitment to the gospel, to holiness and to people. If you use this framework you may be encouraging your group to do another series of studies later.

2. A brief survey of the two letters

Here is a possible selection which will give you a flavour of these letters, though still insufficient to get the whole impact:

1 Thessalonians	1:4–6	2 Thessalonians	2:13–14
	2:10–12		2:15–17
	3:6–10		3:13–18
	5:1–3		
	5:12–15		

3. Studies on the second coming

1 Thessalonians	4:13–15	2 Thessalonians	2:1–3a
	4:16–18		2:3b–12
	5:1–3		(3 studies)
	5:4–8		

4. The theme of encouragement in 1 Thessalonians

1 Thessalonians	1:2–3	3:6–10
	1:6–8	4:13–15
	1:9–10	5:9–11
	2:10–12	5:12–15

These outlines are meant to be springboards for your own ideas, so please do not follow them slavishly. Adapt them for your own use, merge them or ignore them. In any case, much of Thessalonians will go unread if you concentrate only on these short snippets. You as leader will need to read carefully the whole books so that you can refer your group to sections they have not read. It would be wise to read the whole chapter when studying a part of it – the context often throws light on the verses you are looking at.

Finding your way round this book

In our Bible Guides we have developed special symbols to make things easier to follow. Every study therefore has an opening section which is the passage in a nutshell.

The main section is the one that *makes sense of the passage*.

Questions

Every passage also has special questions for personal and group study after the main section. Some questions are addressed to us as individuals, some speak to us as members of our church or home group, while others concern us as members of God's people worldwide. The questions are deliberately designed

▶ to get people thinking about the passage

▶ to apply the text to 'real life' situations

▶ to encourage reflection, discussion and action!

As a group leader you may well discover additional questions that will have special relevance to your group, so look out for these and note them in your preparation time.

Digging deeper

Some passages, however, require an extra amount of explanation, and we have put these sections into two categories. The first kind gives additional background material that helps us to understand something factual. For example, if we dig deeper into the gospels, it helps us to know who the Pharisees were, so that we can see more easily why they related to Jesus in the way they did. These technical sections are marked with a spade.

Important doctrines

The second kind of background section appears with passages which have important doctrines contained in them and which we need to study in more depth if we are to grow as Christians. Special sections that explain them to us in greater detail are marked with a face as above.

Stop and look

This feature gives us the chance to stand back from the action and take stock. It gives a summary of what to look for in the passages we are about to read, and useful background material.

Stop and look: what is 1 Thessalonians all about?

The year is AD 50 (probably). The time: late summer. The place: Athens. Three or so months before, Paul and Silas had fled from Thessalonica by night (see Acts 17:10), obeying the Lord's command to move on when persecution starts (Matthew 10:23), and perhaps hoping that the newly founded Thessalonian church would be spared much more trouble if they left. So they went to preach in Berea.

But it tore Paul's heart-strings to go! How will these young believers survive against such opposition? He prayed and prayed, and longed to see them again (see 2:17–18; 3:5). Eventually, having reached Athens, he sent Timothy to find out how they were. More time passed – more worry and prayer. It takes a month to travel to Thessalonica and back. But then Timothy returned with great news. The church had survived, and was growing strong in faith and love. Paul writes to them, possibly sending Timothy back again with the letter. 'Now I can live, if you are standing firm in the Lord' (*cf.* 1 Thessalonians 3:8).

It was agony for Paul to be separated from them, but a blessing for us. If he had been able to go back himself, he would never have written this marvellous letter, pouring his heart on to paper, voicing his longings and ambitions for these new believers. Satan's plots (2:18) once again backfire – for we too can listen in, as Timothy reads his letter to that new, excited but troubled church.

Some of the topics are special issues about which they had asked him, through Timothy. But other topics are simply the things on Paul's heart, as he reviews his relationship with them and tells them what he would say to every group of new Christians. What's it all about?

There are five themes in 1 Thessalonians:

▶ *How to evangelize.* Paul describes how he preached the gospel in Thessalonica. It is fascinating to have the inside story of Luke's account in Acts 17:1–10. As we watch Paul in action, we are challenged and encouraged about evangelism today.

▶ *How to be a pastor.* One of the strongest impressions this letter leaves is of Paul's *love* for the Thessalonians. He was not just a powerful preacher. He was a loving pastor – or rather, father, nurse, servant and role-model to them. (These are all ways in which he pictures himself here.)

▶ *How to cope with suffering.* The Thessalonian church was born in pain. As soon as they became Christians, they suffered persecution. How do we cope with that kind of thing? Or with suffering of any kind?

▶ *God's priorities for Jesus' disciples.* Paul reminds the Thessalonians of some of the things he taught them while there: fundamental instruction about the basics of Christian discipleship, the absolute 'How do I do it?' of life in the family of God. How do we shape up?

▶ *Get ready for Jesus' return.* This, for Paul, was one of the most basic features of 'life in the family'. Just as he had longed to be reunited with them, so they must look forward to Jesus' coming again. They were worried about a particular issue: what happens to people who have died already, before Jesus comes? Paul replies to that, but broadens it out into a general encouragement to *be ready*. Today, the church has largely forgotten that it is supposed to be waiting for its Lord to come. We need to listen to Paul.

1 Thessalonians 1:1

Hello to God's transplanted people!

Paul writes to them at their address in Thessalonica, but he reminds them of a more important address : they are _in God_.

Years ago when my wife and I knew very little about gardening – in my case, almost nothing! – we fell in love with two beautiful azaleas in the nearby  garden centre and planted them in our front garden, where they promptly keeled over and died. We knew they were azaleas. We didn't know that they were peat-loving plants. We took them from an environment where they were nourished properly and bloomed magnificently; we planted them where they lacked the nutrients and trace elements they needed, and they died.

It was quite the reverse for the Thessalonians – and is for us.

They were still living in Thessalonica – that had not changed. But they had been brought into a different community (*the church*), into a special environment (*in God*) and they were fed with all the nutrients and trace elements (*grace and peace*) necessary for growth and flowering.

A new community: the Lord's people. The word translated *church* (*ekklēsia*) means 'called out'. It can refer to a wide range of gatherings, as in Acts 19:39, 41, but in the New Testament it is primarily one of the ways of describing the

Lord's people – those whom he 'called out' to belong to himself.

This 'calling out' is a very individual matter, and Paul stresses this by writing here, literally, of 'the church of Thessalonians', for the coming of the gospel to Thessalonica did not automatically make all the Thessalonians Christians, but only those who responded to the message.

A new environment: God's transplants. Once upon a time there was nothing more to be said of these Thessalonians than that they lived in this house in that street in Thessalonica, but one day they each gave their allegiance to *another king, Jesus* (Acts 17:7) and immediately they were transplanted into a new soil: they were now *in-God-the-Father-and-the-Lord-Jesus-Christ.* Note the hyphens! This is what Paul implies.

A new nourishment: grace and peace. Ephesians 2:4–6 tells us that mercy, love and grace come to us from God, in Christ, as a life-imparting force.

▶ *Grace* is 'God being gracious', the Father coming to us in all his free, unmerited, saving love and power, sharing himself with us, living in our hearts (John 14:23).

▶ *Peace* is peace with God (Romans 5:1); it is also the peace of a harmonious fellowship (Ephesians 2:14; 4:3–4; James 3:18); peace is also personal life made whole (Mark 5:34; Luke 7:50) and kept secure (Philippians 4:7; 1 Thessalonians 3:16), the self fully matured.

The illustration of a plant in its proper habitat is therefore not a bad one. As God's transplants, we are nourished with his life and transforming power (grace) so as to grow in our three-sided relationship (peace): upwardly, with him, outwardly, with the fellowship, and inwardly, in personal maturity.

Please note: all this is not something future (won't it be nice!); nor is it wishful thinking (wouldn't it be nice!). It is how we are placed now – in the church, in the Father and the Son, in the place of nourishment. Health, growth, flowering, resistance to disease and to withering are the *natural* conditions of the Christian. This is where we are.

Questions

1. 'Grace' is something already given and constantly being given to us (James 4:6), yet we are called to 'grow in grace' (2 Peter 3:18). How do we grow in grace?
2. The church is precious to God (Acts 20:28). Look up the following: Ephesians 1:22; 1 Corinthians 12:14–19; 1 Corinthians 12:20–26; Acts 2:44–45; 4:32–35; 1 Thessalonians 1:7–8. What should we be praying and working for in our own local churches?
3. Write a paragraph each on 'grace' and 'peace', explaining them in simple terms for a non-Christian and non-churchgoer.

Mission Thessalonica: how to plant a church

Acts 17:1–9 tells how Paul came to Thessalonica, and is a model of church-establishing. First, he taught the Scriptures, making the Bible basic to his ministry (verses 1–3); he 'argued his case' (*reasoned*), *explaining* its truths, *proving* his points, *proclaiming* the message in preaching. Secondly, he focused on the Lord Jesus as Messiah/Christ and Saviour (verse 3) and king (verse 7). Thirdly, he addressed people's *minds* initially, by seeking (not to sway emotions but) to 'persuade' (verse 4), to win them over by the truth. Finally, he did not allow suffering to stop him in his tracks: he came to Thessalonica immediately after savage treatment in Philippi (Acts 16:22–24; 1 Thessalonians 2:1–2), but his first thought was to share the gospel (verses 1–2).

THE BASIC
CHRISTIAN LIFE

1 Thessalonians 1:2–10

Stop and look: be a square – or a chair

When we write a letter we have a general idea of what we want to say, and do not allow our letters to get too muddled. All Paul's letters have the same feeling of spontaneity, but always with a clear sense of where he is going next. And, of course, behind and through what Paul wrote ran the inspiring, controlling and guiding of the Holy Spirit (1 Corinthians 2:12–13).

It is helpful, then, to *stop and look* where we are going next.

If we stick with the gardening picture, verses 2–10 work out like this:

1 God's transplants have already produced good fruit (verses 2–3).
2 This good fruit was the product of a sound root (verses 4–5) – the invisible realities of God's choice, the Holy Spirit's power and personal conviction.
3 The model transplant (verse 7) provides good ground-cover. The message which was welcomed (verse 6) spreads in all directions (verse 8).
4 The plant is a hardy perennial, safe even against the coming wrath (verses 9–10).

So there are four sides to the Christian square, or four legs on a Christian chair. Take any leg away and we fall over. To be a *balanced Christian* you need all four sides of the square – or legs of the chair:

▶ evidence (verses 2–3)
▶ spiritual reality (verses 4–5)
▶ experience and response (verses 6–8), and
▶ eternal security (verses 9–10).

24

1 Thessalonians 1:2–3

Delivering the goods

Being a Christian is more than saying so; it is also showing so.

 Here's a person who has frittered opportunities away like the lost son who was left a fortune and squandered it (Luke 15:11–16). 'What's he got to show for it?' people would ask. John the Baptist hammered home the same truth when he demanded that his hearers 'produce fruit in keeping with repentance' (Luke 3:7). In short, spiritual experience must go beyond what we *say* to what we *show*. As he thought about the Thessalonians, there were particular things that moved Paul to thanks and prayer (verse 2). He details them in verse 3 as:

▶ work produced by faith

▶ labour prompted by love

▶ endurance inspired by hope.

The Christian life is an exercise in orienteering – finding one's way through unknown terrain until the goal is reached. But for every step of the way we have not two but three grid references to keep us on track: we look *up* in *faith*, *around* in *love* and *forward* in *hope*.

Faith accepts all parts of our life as coming directly from the hand of God, and trusts him to see us through. It sees even what the world calls 'accidents'– including tragic, shattering accidents – as his gracious appointment for us at that time and place. We cannot be plucked from his hand (John 10:28–29) and nothing can reach us except what he

25

allows to happen (1 Corinthians 10:13).

Love constantly thinks what will benefit the fellowship of the church, and beyond it the unconverted world (2 Peter 1:7). We will live our lives, react to our circumstances and make our decisions only in ways that express this love. 'Loving your neighbour', said Jesus, is like 'loving yourself' (see Mark 12:31). Our love of ourselves is not of the 'hearts going pit-a-pat' variety! No indeed, it is a matter of seeing our needs and meeting them. That's what love is; that's what Jesus did for us; that's the way we are to 'love our neighbours'.

Hope keeps before us the ever fresh possibility that now is the day and hour which no-one knows when we will see the Son of Man coming in clouds (Mark 13:32, 25).

Living in *faith*, *love* and *hope* is no pushover. It is a matter of *work*, *labour*, and *endurance*. Work and labour mean much the same, underlining intensity of effort, readiness to spend strength and accept weariness. The Lord Jesus spoke of *endurance* (Luke 8:15; 21:19), and the New Testament calls us to it (Romans 5:3–4; 8:25). We are not, of course, saved because we do these things; we do them because we are saved. What we say in testimony we must show in results.

Questions

---

1. Paul laid great emphasis on prayer (*e.g.* Romans 1:10; 12:12; 15:30; Ephesians 1:16). So did Jesus (Matthew 5:44; 14:23; Mark 11:24). Make a list of your top ten priorities (work, rest, sleep, eating, *etc.*). Put them in order of value. Where does prayer come? Why?
2. Suppose we knew for certain that Jesus would return tonight. How would we prepare?
3. Our 'neighbours' are worldwide: how can we develop a 'world concern' that is real, not merely a vague feeling of guilt?

1 Thessalonians 1:4–6

Great and lovely secrets

The 'public story' of conversion is how we each accepted the Lord Jesus as our personal Saviour. But there is also a secret story: what God has done to get us there.

One of the great truths of this letter comes for the first time in these verses. Paul is looking back to his arrival in Thessalonica. He recalls things heard and seen.

▶ The word of God was preached ('our gospel came ... with words', verse 5)

▶ the lives of the missionaries were observed ('how we lived among you', verse 5)

▶ the Thessalonians were transformed ('you became imitators', verse 6).

This is effective evangelism, producing changed people. It is the product not just of preaching – the word of God put into *words* – but of the word of God seen in lives that commend the message and provide a model for the converts. But behind this outward evangelism, hidden forces were at work: 'He has chosen you' (verse 4; better, 'he chose you', but literally, 'your election') ... power ... the Holy Spirit ... conviction' (verse 5). Let's look at these.

God's choice. The success of Mission Thessalonica came from a decision made by God. When Paul was in Corinth and opposition seemed to be growing, the Lord Jesus encouraged him to persevere, by saying, 'I have many people in this city' (Acts 18:10). That is to say, they are already mine and they will be gathered to me in personal faith by your ministry. In this way God's choice lies behind every conversion. We come to him because he has chosen us (John 15:16).

The power of God's word. Paul remembers his sense of the power of the word of God as he and others preached it. It was 'not simply with words, but also with power'. Paul and his congregations could hear the word, but he was also aware of power at work whereby the word was *doing* what it was *saying*. He spoke of salvation, of Jesus as Messiah, Saviour and King, and the word was making these truths real in the hearers. This is always what the word of God does. It never fails to do what God wants (Isaiah 55:8–11; Romans 10:17; 1 Thessalonians 2:13).

The Holy Spirit. What power is this which was at work? Not a demonic power, not the force of Paul's personality, not a worked-up hysteria in the hearers, not the effectiveness of eloquence. The third hidden factor which made the mission successful was the Holy Spirit. Genesis 1:1–2 paints a picture which the rest of the Bible explains but never alters: the *hovering* Spirit, waiting to attach himself to the word of God and do what it says, so that when 'God said, "Let there be light" … there was light' (Genesis 1:3).

Conviction. And what did the Spirit do? He gave the hearers 'deep conviction'. Just as he was working with the word to make it effective, so also he was working in the hearers, preparing them to hear, understand, receive and believe the word which they heard.

God's choice and ours

Since we are 'dead' in sins (Ephesians 2:1), we cannot do anything to save ourselves. That is why the Bible says that

▶ 'salvation belongs to God' (Revelation 7:10)

▶ repentance and faith, by which we come to God, are his gifts to us (Acts 5:31; 11:18; Philippians 1:29; 2 Timothy 2:25–26)

▶ his choice of us has to come first (John 15:16; Ephesians 1:4)

▶ no-one can come to Christ unless the Father 'draws' (better 'drags') him (John 6:44).

The list in 1 Thessalonians 1:4–6 starts with divine choice (verse 4), then the effectiveness of God's Word and Spirit, leading to conversion (verse 5), resulting in changed lives (verse 6). It is this observable change that creates confidence in our election or choice by God (2 Peter 1:5–11). God chose us with a view to obedience (Romans 1:5; 1 Peter 1:2), that we should become like Jesus (Romans 8:29) – to keep his commands (1 John 2:3), live like he did (1 John 2:5–6), do what is right (1 John 2:3–8) and love one another (John 13:35). Paul calls this 'faith working by love' (Galatians 5:6; see James 2:14–26).

Does Hebrews 6:4–8, however, imply that people who have been 'enlightened' and have 'tasted' and 'shared' can then 'fall away' and never be recovered? The key to understanding this passage is in the illustration in verses 7–8. Two adjoining pieces of land receive the same blessing of rain, but one produces a 'crop useful', the other 'thorns'. Consequently they have contrasting destinies, 'blessing ... cursed'. It is not, therefore, that those who have truly been saved can fall away – after all, they are saved by divine choice and God is not in the business of changing his mind (Romans 11:29). No, but rather it is possible to go a long way into the things of God and yet not come to that real faith which produces real fruit – like the spies in Numbers 13 who actually entered the land, saw its goodness, breathed its air and ate its fruit but went back to perish in the wilderness. They had wonderful experiences but did not have true faith which obeys and enters into assured possession.

Questions

———————————————————————

1. If evangelism depends on the will of God, the most important thing we can do is to pray that God will do what he alone can do. What practical plans have you for prayer for church growth?
2. Write out in simple terms the gospel you wish to offer. Then each practise, in the group, giving your 'testimony' (not more than two minutes).
3. Paul speaks (verse 5) of the part his manner of life played in winning others for Christ (compare Acts 20:18–19, 33–35.) What sort of lifestyle would impress people around us today?

1 Thessalonians 1:6–8

Mimics and mouths

———————————————

Here are model believers in a model church.

———————————————

So what is a model church like? Look at the way verse 7 begins: 'and so'. Being a model church is *a result of* what verse 6 says. Now look at the way verse 8 begins: 'For' (omitted in NIV). Being a model church (verse 7) is *explained by* what verse 8 says.

First, then, the model church *loves the word of God*. They imitated the apostles and the Lord in welcoming the message (literally, 'the word', verse 6) 'and so ... became a model' (verse 7). It was through the word that they became Christians: the Holy Spirit brought them conviction (verse 5) and in response they welcomed what they heard (verse

6). But also there was the matter of the way they now lived, modelling themselves on Paul and Jesus (verse 6).

Secondly, the model church *perseveres with the word of God* in a way that can be explained only by the presence and work of the Holy Spirit (verse 6). In his parable of the sower, the Lord Jesus teaches that when the word of God comes, testing comes as well. Satan never leaves the word of God alone (Mark 4:15, 17, 19). Luke 8:15 teaches that fruitfulness results from *hearing and holding* the word with endurance. It was not persecution as such, then, that made them models but that when their welcome of the word was tested they persevered – not with gritted teeth but with such joy in spiritual truth that it had to be of the Holy Spirit.

Thirdly, they *trumpeted the word of God* (verse 8). Remember the 'For' verse 8 starts with. They are a model church 'because' 'the message [the word] rang out from you'. There were two sides to their testimony:

- they told the truth – the gospel
- *your faith in God has become known*: they also told how to respond to the gospel in simple trust in the Lord Jesus for salvation – like the Philippian jailer in Acts 16:30–31.

The hymn says:

> Just as I am, you will receive,
> Will welcome, pardon, cleanse, relieve,
> Because your promise I believe:
> O Lamb of God, I come.

The first two lines 'tell the truth': the gospel of grace, its open invitation and lovely promises. The second two lines tell how to respond: by believing and coming. That is the testimony of the model church.

Questions

1. Is the word of God sufficiently central in our public and personal worship? How can we make it more so?
2. What ways do you find effective for hearing and welcoming the word of God in daily devotions?
3. How would you go about encouraging others – both converted and unconverted – in Bible reading?
4. What is faith? Consider the people, events and even objects that we trust and put our faith in. Compare these with faith in God.

Focus on the Bible

Paul put the word of God at the centre of his ministry, and this is nowhere seen more clearly than in his last letter, 2 Timothy. Knowing that he is about to die (2 Timothy 4:6), his charge to Timothy is that

► while others are turning away (1:15) he must 'hold fast the pattern of sound words' (1:13–14)

► while others are denying central truth (2:17–18) he must 'work at the word' (2:15)

► while all around there is moral breakdown (3:1–5), he must 'continue' (3:14) in the God-breathed word (3:15–17); and

► while others are preaching alternative 'gospels' (4:3–4), he must 'preach the word ... do the work of an evangelist' (4:2–5).

The Lord Jesus loved the word of God. When the crunch came (Matthew 26:51–54) and he could so easily have

prayed for angelic deliverance, his overriding concern was
rather that the Scriptures be fulfilled; and at the end, racked
with the thirst which was one of the awful sufferings of the
crucified, he said, 'I thirst', not to ease his own pain but in
order that the Scripture should be fulfilled (John 19:28).

1 Thessalonians 1:9–10

Happy ever after!

They turned, they served, they waited.

Conversion is very simple: we trust
Jesus and are saved. Long ago Christians used to say that we 'received the
Lord Jesus into our hearts as our own
personal Saviour', and that is still the best description of a
true conversion. But however simple it was – and however
little we knew about the Jesus we received – eternal issues
were raised and settled at that moment.

Notice the contrasts in these verses:

▶ There is either the 'living and true God' or 'idols'.
There is no halfway house, no 'I suppose'. Those who
are not committed to him who is true are committed
to those who are false (2 Timothy 4:3–4).

▶ There is either 'the coming wrath' or safety in 'Jesus,
who rescues'; there is no middle-ground, no 'Well,
maybe'.

Conversion involves commitment: out of one camp into
the other. Colossians 1:13 rightly sees this 'moving house' as
the work of God, because all our salvation is always from

him (1 Corinthians 1:27–31). But at conversion the decision is in our court: 'you turned'. Yet that turning was an eternal turning-point, and from that moment onward we were in the care of the Rescuer. In verse 10, 'who rescues' is a present participle and therefore an ongoing activity. It is not, however, that the work of rescue is still somehow incomplete, but that he is 'ever the Rescuer'.

The resurrection is the God-given proof of what Jesus did on the cross.

▶ In his death, Jesus cleared all our debt before God. He endured the cross until his holy conscience told him he could claim, 'It is finished' (John 19:28–30).

▶ But does God think so? Does the God whom our sin has offended think the offence has been erased? Yes, indeed! He showed his satisfaction with what his Son did on the cross by raising him from the dead. As Romans 4:25 says, 'he was handed over [to death] because of our sins; he was raised because of our justification', *i.e.*, because his death really did clear our account with God.

All this is yours through the simple fact that 'you turned'.

Questions

1. The news of the Thessalonians' conversion spread (verse 9) because they themselves spread it (verse 8). Do we find faith-sharing hard? What can we do to be more vocal? What do verses 9–10 suggest the Thessalonians said about themselves?
2. What 'idols' capture people today worldwide? What alternative do we offer?
3. Jesus was very clear about 'hell': see Matthew 10:28; 13:49–50; 18:8; 23:33; 25:46; Mark 3:29; Luke 12:5; 16:23. What do we make of this? Has it a place in our testimony?

2

COMMITMENT TO THE GOSPEL, TO HOLINESS AND TO PEOPLE

1 Thessalonians 2:1–16

Stop and look: more 'saying and showing'

Effective gospel-sharing depends on the sort of life we live as well as on the message we share. Very small words are often very important. The Greek of chapter 2 opens with just such a word, 'For' or 'Because'. Paul launches into an explanation. What is he explaining? He has been remembering how he came to Thessalonica (1:9) and the wonderful results that followed (1:9–10): their decision ('you turned'), commitment ('to God from idols'), service ('to serve'), perseverance ('to wait'). In other words, these were genuine conversions, not a flash in the pan but permanently changed lives with new loyalty (to God), new lifestyle (slave-service) and new expectations (the 'Son from heaven').

Wouldn't we like to know the secret of such effectiveness in winning others?

The secret is simple to find but costly to practise.

▶ In verses 2–4, Paul recalls how he and his colleagues shared the all-important truth ('his gospel') in the situation that demanded perseverance ('we had … suffered'; 'we dared to tell') and holy ('not … impure') lives and approved 'hearts'.

▶ In verse 8, they shared 'the gospel of God' and at the same time their 'lives … because you had become so dear to us'. Paul's commitment to the gospel was equalled by his loving commitment to people. He was not looking for scalps to hang on his belt.

▶ In verses 10–12, in his task of 'urging' (literally 'bearing witness'), Paul could speak of himself as 'holy, righteous … blameless'.

In summary, then, it was this combination of commitment *to the gospel*, *to personal holiness* and *to people* that produced such lasting results.

Paul presents this important truth in a very careful way:

▶ He begins with the word of God (the gospel) and its messengers (verses 1–4).

▶ He ends (verses 13–16) with the word of God and its hearers.

In between he offers two illustrations of true ministry:

▶ verses 5–9, the nurse and her babies, and

▶ verses 10–12, the father and his children.

1 Thessalonians 2:1–4

The trustee

Paul is 'approved by God to be entrusted with the gospel' (verse 4). Can we make the same claim?

The gospel is the truth about Jesus (Romans 1:9) and about God's grace (Acts 20:24). It is not something anyone can take up and prattle. It is (verse 2, literally) 'the gospel of God'; it belongs to him and he entrusts it to those he approves (verse 4). Effective gospel-sharing is not just knowing the facts; it is a matter of qualifying to be a trustee.

A trustee relies on God for strength. Paul had suffered savagely at Philippi (Acts 16:23–24). Indeed, over and over again in his gospel work he had experienced opposition and injury (Acts 13:50; 14:5–6, 19, 22). How could he face it all again in Thessalonica? Only 'with the help of our God'. 'We emboldened ourselves in our God' (verse 2, literally).

A trustee presents the good news simply: 'to tell you his gospel' (verse 2). He uses the ordinary verb 'to speak, say, chat' (Acts 11:19–20). The simplicity of the gospel (1 Corinthians 15:3–4) was matched by simplicity in the telling.

A trustee accepts personal risks: 'in spite of strong opposition' (verse 2). This was Paul to a T, always on the alert for a chance to tell of Jesus; no doubt counting the cost but ever ready to pay it. He couldn't see a crowd without wanting to talk to them – even when the situation was ugly and he was himself in chains (Acts 21:33–39), facing torture (22:24). See the same readiness in Acts 18:14; 19:29–30.

A trustee is sincere. 'What shall I say?' (verse 3). The answer is, nothing but the truth. 'What am I out for? To get people into my power? To use them simply as a means for my own satisfaction?' The answer is, 'Share the gospel for their advantage, not for mine.' 'How shall I go about it? Shall I try to con people into decisions or leave it to the truth to convince them?' The answer is, 'Use nothing but the persuasion of the truth.' See Acts 17:1–4, 11–12, as an illustration of Paul's trusteeship.

Finally, a trustee has a heart's desire to please God (verse 4).

Questions

1. Paul says bluntly that Mission Thessalonica was 'not a failure' (2:1). But often this is what our evangelism is. What lessons can we learn – and apply – to make it more effective?
2. Suffering is a great problem, but Paul seems to accept it without questioning (2:2). How does his example help us? See also Mark 4:1–20; Romans 5:3–5; James 1:2–4; 1 Peter 4:12–14.
3. In what ways are we tempted to please people rather than God? How do we seek to please God?

Bible translations

More recent translations of the Bible often omit small connecting words (like the 'For' with which Paul begins verse 1). It is a good plan to keep an older translation by you just to check on things like this. The older translations are often more reliable on seemingly small points; the newer ones score on making a biblical meaning more easily understood. Alongside the New International Version, Good News Bible, Revised English Bible and New Revised Standard Version, try using the Authorized (King James) Version, Revised Version, Revised Authorized (New King James) Version and the New American Standard Bible.

Concordances

A concordance lists every passage in which a word occurs. By looking up other passages we can begin to grasp the range of meaning of the words in our Bibles. The older translations tend to be more consistent in using the same English word for the same Hebrew word (in the Old Testament) and Greek word (in the New), while the new translations often use a great variety of English equivalents in an attempt to make the meaning of a passage plainer. *Young's Analytical Concordance* and *Strong's Exhaustive Concordance* (based on the Authorized Version) list the English words under their Hebrew and Greek equivalents and are therefore particularly useful to us.

In the present passage:

▶ In verse 2, 'dared' is translated in Acts 9:27 as

'preached fearlessly'; 9:28, 'speaking boldly'; 26:26, 'speak freely'; Ephesians 6:20, 'declare fearlessly'. It combines clarity and courage.

▶ In verse 3, 'impure motives' is 'uncleanness'. See Romans 1:24, 'sexual impurity'; Galatians 5:24, 'impurity'. Sexual sin is well to the fore in this word. It points here to the need for absolute purity of relationships between Christians and those with whom they share the gospel.

1 Thessalonians 2:5–9

Tender loving care

Work, self-sacrifice and suffering all make sense when you love people.

We must start by restoring the opening word 'For' to verse 5. Paul has claimed (verse 4) that he and his team spoke as people of whom God approved and  whose priority was to please him. Verses 5–9 explain what this involves. The passage is shaped like an old-fashioned egg-timer with two glass bowls joined by a narrow neck. Verse 5 to the beginning of verse 7 are all negative (what Paul did not do); verses 8 and 9 are positive (what Paul did do, and did gladly). The second half of verse 7, the illustration of the nurse, is the narrow neck of the egg-timer, holding the section together.

Look at the illustration, then (verse 7b). Paul focuses on the highest example of unself-seeking love that the world knows, the mother with her little ones. Indeed, it may be that he goes one step further, for the word translated 'mother' could equally well – maybe even better – be translated 'nurse'. Professionally, a true nurse will give herself, with all her training and skills, to her charges. But suppose those charges are (literally) 'her very own children'? All that professional skill is raised to the nth degree by the maternal relationship. What a picture of Christian ministry!

And this is evangelism! Yet Paul says nothing about large-scale campaigning, addressing meetings, pulpits, halls, advertising. It is not that these things do not have their time and place; it is that they are not the heart of the matter. Paul's was personal, tender, caring evangelism, love-evangelism, arising not out of a special evangelistic gift but out of the universal Christian characteristic that 'we loved you so much' (verse 8).

A fourfold denial (verses 5–7a)

1 He did not flatter or have a secret agenda (*mask*) of self-gain, work for praise, or stand on his proper dignity as an apostle. Never once (verse 5)! 'Flattery' here means buttering people up to gain an advantage over them. It is more, therefore, than mere flattery; it is a deliberate ploy in order to gain one's own ends.

2 'Greed' goes a little deeper. Flattery might be aimed at some particular gain, but greed speaks of a nature that is never satisfied, always out for more, 'covetousness'. Flattery would be open, but 'covetousness' is an ulterior motive.

3 Equally insidious is the secret longing to be praised. Surely the Thessalonians did praise Paul for bringing the gospel to them, and surely it was right that they should. It is in this way that we rightly affirm the ministry of those who have been a blessing to us, and our affirmation is a blessing to them. But it is quite another matter to work for praise, to be dependent on it, to bask in its sunshine.

4 He also gave up what could have been rightfully his, whatever he could well have claimed as an apostle of

Christ (verse 7). Obviously here he is thinking of support in money or kind, imposing himself as a 'burden'. There would have been nothing wrong in this (1 Corinthians 9:3–12), and he had no problem about accepting support from his established churches (Philippians 4:14–16), but to him it would have obscured (even damaged) the love-motive if he had made enquirers and those just barely in Christ responsible for his upkeep.

Three positives (verses 8–9)

1 *His yearning and love.* 'We loved you' (verse 8) is the feeling of love, yearning as felt by a lover. 'Delighted' expresses the satisfaction the lover experiences in serving the loved one, the love that reaches out. 'Dear to us' is love as centred on the beloved object.
2 *His total self-giving to those to whom he ministered* (verse 8): 'not only the gospel … but our lives as well', literally 'our very selves'.
3 *The sacrificial effort he was prepared to make in ministry* (verse 9): 'toil and hardship'. He supported himself lest anything obscure the freeness of the gospel, presented in loving, self-giving and costly self-sacrifice.

Questions

1. To what extent does the teaching of verses 5–9 apply also to us? For example, is our workplace to be like Paul's, an evangelistic ministry?
2. How can we cultivate the self-effacing, unself-seeking humility the apostle showed – and his love for those around him in Thessalonica?
3. If people praise us, how should we respond? How should we feel? What should we say? How should we act?

Apostles

When Paul speaks of 'apostles' (in the plural) in verse 7, he may be using the word in its occasional general sense as those sent by the church to minister to others (as in Acts 14:4, 14; Romans 16:7; 2 Corinthians 8:23; Philippians 2:15). In this sense Paul would include Silas and Timothy (1:1) with himself as emissaries from the church at Antioch (Acts 13:1–3; 15:40). Alternatively, since Paul commonly speaks of himself as 'we' in this letter, he may have slipped unconsciously into the plural, 'apostles'.

It was a recognized right of apostles, apparently, to look for support in their wide-ranging work (1 Corinthians 9:3–13), and in this sense of the word the apostles were a unique band, 'the twelve' (Mark 3:13–18; Acts 6:2). Revelation 21:14 marks their uniqueness in that their names are on the foundations of the heavenly Jerusalem. Paul underlines the uniqueness of the apostle in two ways: first, the apostle's calling included seeing the Lord Jesus (1 Corinthians 9:1); secondly, the apostle has an inspired role in communicating God's truth (1 Corinthians 2:12–13): the Holy Spirit grants understanding (verse 12), and imparts the words to be used (verse 13a), so that 'spiritual truths' are perfectly expressed in matching 'spiritual words' (verse 13b). Paul registers the same claim in 1 Thessalonians 2:13. Apart from the (to me, outside) possibility that James is called an apostle in Galatians 1:19, there is no New Testament reference to an apostle carrying on a permanently settled ministry in a local church.

1 Thessalonians 2:10-12

To encourage, to comfort and to teach

Here is typical biblical fatherliness as one huge aspect of pastoral care.

Wouldn't it be great to be as confident about the example we set in our lives and work as Paul was? He had no doubt what people would say about him: 'You are witnesses (verse 10) ... 'you know' (verse 11). Neither has he any doubt what God would think of him: 'and so is God' (verse 10). He didn't call others into anything he had not reached himself (verse 12, 'lives worthy of God').

He makes it specially the duty of a 'father' to set standards by word and action (verses 10–12). What he says in these verses applies first in the home; it is only because it is true of the home that it can become an illustration of what should be true in ministry. It is because fathers should be like this that Paul can make them a model for his ministry.

And yet there is nothing about the father *saying* anything until we get to verse 12. So very often our anxiety that our children should be the best for God far outstrips our personal commitment to being the best for God. Not for Paul! Not in the Bible!

When Paul spoke to the Ephesian church leaders, he said, 'Guard yourselves and all the flock' (Acts 20:28). Do you notice the order in which he lists their responsibilities? Themselves first! If they are not caring for their own spiritual welfare, how can they care for anyone else? If their daily devotions (their Bible-reading and prayer) lapse, what reality would there be in their advice to others? If they are careless about fellowship and lax in coming to the Lord's table, how can they commend to others what they treat as unimportant?

This holiness is public ('you are witnesses', verse 10). It is also like the wording on seaside rock – it goes right through to the centre as something that God sees (verse 10). It is practical and practised: 'we were' (verse 10) is more accurately 'we proved ourselves to be' – we set out to be like this and you saw it in us.

But what does the father/leader actually do? Our fatherly practice is often far too negative; and it must have been so in Paul's day too, because elsewhere he warns fathers against nagging their children (Ephesians 6:4, 'exasperate'; Colossians 3:21, 'embitter', meaning 'pester, harass'). But here all is positive. In verse 10, Paul describes the father/leader's ministry in the following ways:

▶ setting objectives for their children and those they lead by 'encouraging' (which includes 'exhorting' and 'pleading' in its meaning; see Romans 12:1; Ephesians 4:1; Philemon 9)

▶ picking them up and dusting them down by appropriate 'comforting' or 'consoling' (John 11:19, 31), offering the handkerchief for tears and the bandage for hurts

▶ affirming the truth: 'urging' is literally 'testifying', and in the New Testament this always means 'attesting', 'bearing witness to the truth' (Acts 26:22; Galatians 5:3; Ephesians 4:17).

The father/leader addresses the *will* by exhorting, the *feelings* by consoling and the *mind* by affirming what is true.

Paul then underlines three things: God's call, kingdom and glory.

God's call. In Paul, 'calling' (*e.g.* Romans 8:30) is like 'conscription'; it is not an invitation to consider a possibility but a sovereign appointment to a new position. In many countries a period of service in the armed forces is still compulsory. When a young person receives call-up papers, he or she does not respond by saying, 'How very kind of His or Her Majesty to invite me to consider joining the armed forces! I will give it my close consideration and let my sovereign know.' The arrival of the papers at once changes his or her whole life. The old has become new (2 Corinthians 5:17–18); though the young person has much to learn, this civilian has now become a soldier, no longer a free agent but 'under authority'. So, God has 'conscripted' us into possession of all he has done for us in and through the Lord Jesus Christ.

God's kingdom. But, alongside their call, the father reminds his children of their membership of God's kingdom where they give their loyal obedience to 'another king, one called Jesus' (Acts 17:7). In other words, the illustration of earthly conscription is exact. Conscripts now have a primary duty to consider the good of their country, to give loyalty to its government in a very committed way and to obey orders. Paul puts this in the forefront of the life empowered by grace in 2 Timothy 2:1, 3–4, and he often uses military illustrations (Romans 6:13, 'instruments' is 'weapons'; 13:12; Ephesians 6:11–13). The central idea of kingdom membership is obedience springing out of loyalty.

God's glory. The third aspect of the father's encouragement takes up the theme of *glory*. He prompts his children to live looking forward, to consider the inheritance that awaits them and to live in the light of it. In Philippians 3:20 Paul speaks of our heavenly 'citizenship'. He means two things. First, we are already citizens of that heavenly city (Hebrews 12:23), possessing its rights, under its laws. Secondly, we are called to live here as if we were already there – as he says in 1:1, though still 'in Thessalonica' we must live as those 'in God the Father'. 1 John 2:28 – 3:3 offers a perfect summary: wonderful things lie ahead; they are our sure and certain hope. So we must live now as those who possess great treasures and long to please a great Lord.

Questions

1. In what ways does it matter what people think of us, and in what ways does it not matter?
2. How do we know the will of God in order to obey it? Weigh up the value of church teaching, truths in the Bible, advice of friends, inner conviction, other influences. Put them in order of importance.
3. These verses apply directly to fathers, but they apply by way of illustration to church leaders. In what way do they also apply to each of us in our care and concern for one another?

1 Thessalonians 2:13–16

The big issue

Accepting or rejecting the word of God.

Acts 17:1–4 is a cameo of Paul as a missionary. In one word, his message was 'Jesus' as revealed in the Scriptures. This was the thrust of his teaching while he was in Thessalonica. Now, looking back, he has much to be grateful for, and he has already mentioned the way the Thessalonians are living out the life of Christ in their pagan environment (1 Thessalonians 1:2). When, however, he goes right back to fundamentals, this is the way he expresses his thanksgiving (verses 13–14a): he brought them the word of God, they *recognized* it as such, accepted it, believed it, and found it to be effective in their lives. This is what being a Christian is all about.

We do not, of course, worship the Bible. The wise men worshipped only the child, but 'when they saw the star, they were overjoyed' – because the star pointed to him (Matthew 2:11–12). To us the Bible is that star. Without it we would not know about him in any meaningful way. We certainly would not know him personally, or be able to 'grow in the grace and knowledge of our Lord and Saviour' (2 Peter 3:18).

This is the fundamental topic which occupies Paul in the present section.

Certainly, from first to last, the Bible is the 'word' of its human authors. Matthew has his crisp, businessman's style; Luke writes like the cultured, educated man he was. Compare the earthy James with the more imaginative John, or Paul with Peter. Every bit of the Bible is coloured by the distinct personalities of its authors. But Amos (typical of the prophets) opened his book with the double statement, 'The words of Amos ... This is what the LORD says ...' (Amos 1:1, 3). Paul claims that the apostolic word arose from wisdom imparted by the Holy Spirit and was couched in words taught by the Holy Spirit, so as to give perfect spiritual expression to spiritual truth (1 Corinthians 2:12–13). Peter brackets Paul's letters with 'the other Scriptures' (2 Peter 3:16). Of course, it stands to reason that the divine Author is more important than the human author, and this is why Paul corrects our perspective on the Bible by saying, 'not ... the word of men, but ... the word of God' (verse 13). This is why the Bible is such a 'star'.

This is also the reason Paul can say that 'the word ... is at work in you' (verse 13). It is the word of him who 'said, "Let there be light," and there was light' (Genesis 1:3), who 'spoke, and it came to be; he commanded, and it stood firm' (Psalm 33:9): the word that can never be ineffective (Isaiah 55:8–11).

How important it is that we know how to respond to this potent word! Paul uses three verbs:

▶ *Received*. This verb means to accept a tradition handed down on authority (1 Corinthians 15:1; Galatians 1:9).

The authoritative source is, of course, the Lord himself, from whom the word came to us through his hand-picked messengers (Acts 10:40; Ephesians 3:4–5).

► *Accepted.* The second verb speaks of the welcome the word was given by the hearers. It was not, so to speak, an overnight guest in their ears, but was welcomed right into mind and heart (Luke 8:12, 15).

► *Believe.* The third verb expresses the response of faith accorded to the trustworthy word, and to the Lord of whom it speaks.

What then did the effective word of God do as it worked in the Thessalonian believers? There were two results.

First, they conformed their lives to the general Christian pattern set by the existing churches (verse 14a). This is not, of course, to turn from the word of God to human traditions. It would not be safe to follow the churches except in so far as they follow God's word. But sensibly, Paul recognizes that the main lines of scriptural life and behaviour have already been worked out, and that what is new is almost certain to be wrong. The individual nature of our response to the Lord Jesus does not give us leave to be individualistic.

But, secondly, Paul writes about suffering (verse 14). It is the same point that we noted in 2:2 (see above): there is no such thing as an untested faith. Perseverance is one of the marks of a true trust in Jesus.

Questions

1. In the light of Paul's explanation of how we should respond to God's word, how does our Bible reading match up? How often do we read it? How do we respond to it? As a group, discuss different methods of Bible-reading and aids found helpful.
2. The testings and trials of life so often seem untimely and

purposeless, and we get troubled about them. Look at John 10:28–29; Romans 5:3–5; 1 Corinthians 10:13. God always has purposes in mind, though they are not always what we think or want. How do we react to these verses? How do you respond to someone who says life is purposeless?

3. Paul was not afraid to speak of the awful results of unbelief. How can we follow his example, with the same clarity and sensitivity? And should we do so? Has the wrath of God a place in our evangelism?

Paul and the Jews

Some interpret verses 14–16 as an anti-Semitic outburst which seems to them to contradict the tenderness Paul expresses elsewhere (Romans 9:1–3; 10:1; 11:14) about his fellow-Jews. But, as we have seen, these verses are just *factual*. Paul does no more than record the fact that rejection of the word of God can only leave those who reject it without hope of salvation, without forgiveness and without escape from wrath (Hebrews 2:3). That's the way it is. There is no other way of salvation for anyone except in Jesus, and apart from him there is no shield against 'the wrath of a sin-hating God'.

Do not read these verses in an angry, embittered voice; read them (as I would suppose Paul wrote them) with tears. This is no vitriolic outburst, but a grim analysis applicable to all who reject the word of God: their deeds, past and present (15a), their position before God (15b), their hostility to people even in respect of the gospel (15c, 16a), the direction in which all this is moving (16b), and the inevitable result (16c).

3

PAUL'S LOVE
FOR THE
THESSALONIANS

1 Thessalonians 2:17 – 4:8

Stop and look: the world, the flesh and the devil

They say that all the world loves a lover. It is, of course, simply not true. But it is true that love stories are big business. In that case we are in business with this section of 1 Thessalonians. It is the story of Paul's love affair with the Thessalonian church. We can subdivide it like this:

2:17–20. *Frustration.* Paul loved his Thessalonians so deeply that to be away from them was like a bereavement. In verse 17, 'torn away', means literally 'made orphans', like children bereaved of their parents. His heart never left Thessalonica; he had an 'intense longing' to get back (verse 17). Even the second coming of the Lord Jesus would lose its *joy* (verses 19–20) if the Thessalonians weren't there too. For him, they are part of the great 'hope'.

3:1–5. *Timothy's mission.* The story of Paul's love continues. He accepted the experience of aloneness in a strange city (verse 1) and the loss of a cherished brother and colleague (verse 2) in the interests of their spiritual welfare. That they should experience trials (verse 3) without his support was something he could 'stand ... no longer' (verse 5).

3:6–10. *Timothy's return.* To hear Timothy's report that the Thessalonians were staunch in 'faith and love' for the Lord, for each other and for Paul was 'good news' (verse 6). The word Paul uses here is the one used for telling the 'good news' of the gospel. To hear good news of them was like hearing the gospel for the first time! It was just the encouragement Paul needed (verse 7). It was like coming back to life (verse 8).

3:11–13. *Joy and relief issue in prayer.* Here is a slight over-paraphrase of verses 11–12: 'But when all is said and done, it is for God to direct ... and for God to increase.' This is the point of Paul's prayer. He has been lovingly fretting and fuming because he is not with the Thessalonians. How essential it is to remember that God is with them! They are God's responsibility; they are in his hands, and they couldn't be in a better place. They do not have Paul, but they have two great guardian Friends, two minds with but a single thought – for Paul speaks here of 'our God and Father' and 'our Lord Jesus', but he binds the two together into unity by using a singular verb. In 1:1 we noted that Father and Son were united by a single preposition, 'in'. In their unity they provided the perfect 'soil' for God's transplanted people, with all the nutrients and trace elements they would ever need. Here the singular verb makes the Two a single, mighty, divine force for care and welfare in all the hazards of life.

4:1–8. *Paul's conclusion.* Literally, he writes: 'To take things forward, therefore' (verse 1). Paul is not with them, but God is. His purpose is that they should be 'blameless and holy' (3:13). What then does the future hold? 'It is God's will that you should be sanctified' (4:3). Holiness is a divine work (3:13); it is also a human objective (3:3). To this end God gives his Holy Spirit (4:8). Note how the reference to the Holy Spirit rounds off the reference to Father and Son in 3:11. The Holy Trinity is on our side.

This long section tells the story of Paul's love for the Thessalonians (and us, his present-day Thessalonians): how he longed for them, agonized over them, rejoiced to hear of their well-being, reminded himself and them of their sufficiency in God, and summoned them to holiness. But in each section, as well as telling the story of his love, Paul raises an important spiritual issue. The sections come together like this:

A   2:17–20, the reality of Satan and his purpose to hinder (verse 18)

    B   3:1–5, Christians battling (verses 2–4)

    B¹   3:6–10, Christians overcoming (verses 7–8)

A¹   3:11–4:8, the reality of God and his purpose of holiness (3:13; 4:3, 7–9)

This diagram is the basis on which we will now look at some of the details of the section.

1 Thessalonians 2:17–20

Your enemy the devil

The word of God is always opposed, and the same spiritual opponent constantly watches out to threaten Christians and to bar their progress.

Satan our enemy

We must not get obsessed with Satan. The Bible does not encourage paying him too much attention. Its references to the devil are in fact comparatively few and far between. In all his letters together, Paul mentions 'Satan' only nine or ten times. The Tempter ought not, therefore, to bulk large in our consideration or conversation. There is one Bible fact about Satan, however, on which we must dwell and be as clear as we can: Satan is not a free agent, either in his choice of subjects for his attention or in the extent to which he can exercise his evil power against them. We find this illustrated in Job 1 – 2. Satan is subordinate to God; Satan works only as God directs and within the limits he imposes; Satan is the opponent of what is good and godly.

▶ Satan is a powerful being (John 12:31; 2 Corinthians 4:4), cunning (2 Corinthians 11:3, 14), deceitful (Ephesians 6:11; 2 Thessalonians 2:9), lying (John 8:44), making false claims (Luke 4:6), wicked (Ephesians 6:16).

▶ Satan opposes the word of God (Matthew 13:19), perverts its meaning (Matthew 4:6), blinds the minds of unbelievers (2 Corinthians 4:4; 2 Timothy 2:26), seeks the downfall of believers (Acts 5:3; 2 Corinthians 2:11), afflicts (2 Corinthians 12:7).

▶ These references hardly scratch the surface of the nature and activity of Satan, but they are all held firmly in the grip of a verse that does not even mention him at all: 'No temptation has seized you except what is common to man. And God is faithful; he will not let you be tempted beyond what you can bear. But when you are tempted, he will also provide a way out so that you can stand up under it' (1 Corinthians 10:13).

Satan stopped us

Even though Paul's return to Thessalonica from Athens meant days of walking, maybe often through inhospitable parts, or the discomforts of sea travel (Acts 17:15), it seems a comparatively simple thing. But *Satan stopped us* (verse 18). How did Satan stop him? If it was important for us to know, we would have been told; since we are not told it cannot be important. But, for example, did the bond Jason and the others signed to keep the peace (Acts 17:9) include a clause forbidding Paul to be in Thessalonica? Or did Paul have an otherwise unrecorded bout of ill-health? But if it was any such thing, why does he not say so? Because what is important is not *how* Satan hindered him but *that* Satan hindered him. Christian service is always a conflict; there is always a mighty and malign power laying roadblocks, booby-traps and anti-personnel mines. That's the way it is.

Yet there is a deeper thing to say. Satan operates only at divine direction and within divine bounds. If Satan was the instrument, the Lord was the Agent. It was he who used Satan to stop Paul. Paul felt that unless he was there the Thessalonians could not possibly stand firm, hold the faith, stick it out. They needed him; without him, what were they? But he was quite wrong. They did stand firm, they did hold the faith, they did stick it out (3:6–7). Paul's tender loving care in person would have been a bonus, but it was not a necessity.

Is this what God wanted the Thessalonians to learn – how

to lean directly on him and prove his sufficiency? Is it what he wanted Paul to learn – that it is one thing to take our responsibilities seriously, but another thing to forget that there is a living, loving, caring God, never forgetting, ever present, totally sufficient?

Questions

1. It is not good to think or talk too much about Satan, but it might be helpful to share about temptations. How do they come? How can we avoid them? How can we practise the way of escape?
2. How can we store up the word of God in our minds and memories so as to have it ready when we need it?
3. Does Paul's love for his Thessalonians say anything to us about our lukewarmness? What is the secret of enthusiastic Christian relationships, mutual care and concern?

1 Thessalonians 3:1–5

In the arena

Sometimes Satan's forces drop on us like unexpected paratroopers out of a clear blue sky; sometimes they lie in ambush; sometimes they come openly marching with flags flying.

The word translated 'unsettled' (verse 3) comes from a verb used of a dog wagging its tail. And since dogs do this because they sense that it pleases, the verb moves on to mean 'to entice'; but also, from the tail-wagging movement, it came to mean 'to shake, agitate, perturb'. Aren't words interesting!

There is one particular thing which 'entices' people away from the path of truth and 'shakes' them out of their confidence and 'perturbs' their peace of mind. It is the sudden onset of trouble: what we call 'the problem of suffering'. An elderly man I spoke to 'used to attend church until, one year, my wife and only child died within six months of each other, and after that it didn't seem worth bothering'. We can all identify with that feeling, and we all know others with that same reaction.

This is what Paul feared for his Thessalonians. He left them in the thick of opposition and ugly situations (Acts 17:5–7). Whether he wished it or not, though he probably made the Lord's command his guide (Matthew 10:23), his fellow-Christians hustled him away (Acts 17:10). But he knew that the persecution of the church continued after he had left, and his heart bled for his suffering friends. Would they be 'enticed' away from the Lord, 'shaken' in their faith and 'perturbed' in mind and heart?

What would Paul have said to the troubled Thessalonians had he been with them? What would he say, on the basis of this passage, to us, his present-day Thessalonians?

First, he would say, hold on to the way of *faith* (verses 3, 5). That is to say, when trouble comes let your first port of call be not the question 'Why?' but the affirmation, right in the thick of it all, 'I believe in God the Father Almighty ... and in his Son ... and in the Holy Spirit ...' Circumstances have changed, but God has not. I think it is in his sci-fi novel *Voyage to Venus* that C. S. Lewis has one of the beings living there say to his space-traveller, Ransom, about the Great God whom they know as Maleldil: 'He is not a leaf to be blown off course or a twig to be trodden underfoot.' In other words, no power can intrude on his purposes; he is not a dead object but the living God.

Next, Paul would speak to them and us about *duty*. He says in verse 3 that 'we were destined for' these trials. He uses the same verb when he is himself in the soup – in prison, probably in Rome (Philippians 1:16, translated 'put here'). One writer suggests, very suitably, 'on duty'. If we are 'destined' for troubles, then this is the appointed sphere of our discipleship. Don't we all say things like: 'If only life were easier!' 'If only I had more money!' 'If only my family weren't so difficult!' 'If only my work were more congenial!'? 'Then I would be a more committed Christian, I would undertake this or that or the other for the Lord.' But it's not like that – and never will be till we are home in heaven.

Paul's third word to the troubled touches on *knowledge*. 'When we were with you, we kept telling you that we would be persecuted' (verse 4). In other words they were forewarned and therefore should have been forearmed. So should we. Trouble may often alarm us, but it should never surprise us. Jesus forewarned us (John 16:33), and so did Paul (Acts 14:22; 2 Timothy 3:12) and Peter (1 Peter 5:10). James even calls us to be joyful over trouble, because it is God's sure-fire way forward to maturity (James 1:2–4). Peter reminds us not to think trials are 'strange' but rather to see them as opportunities for Christlikeness (1 Peter 4:12–13).

Questions

1. Paul sent Timothy to 'strengthen … your faith' (verse 2). The verb means 'to buttress', 'to support a wall'. What do you find are the best 'buttresses' for faith?
2. How can we most helpfully minister to ourselves, to our fellow-Christians and to our non-Christian friends in times of trouble? Don't forget to think about Christians in other countries, especially those suffering persecution.
3. The accepted wisdom of the world aims for success and the avoidance of suffering. On that basis, to be persecuted must be a sign of failure. Is there any truth in this? If not, why can't the world see it?

1 Thessalonians 3:6–10

Winning through

Our task is to learn to live in Christ, not to escape from all problems.

 Maybe we would not have been surprised if Timothy had come back to Paul with news of some great gatherings for prayer, seeking the almighty power of the Lord Jesus in a ministry of deliverance, casting Satan out. After all, that was their core problem, wasn't it? Wasn't the animosity of Satan the 'real' explanation of the hostility of the Jews and the readiness of the town 'rent-a-mob' (Acts 17:5) to stir trouble against the infant church? Why fuss around with the monkey when you can go for the organ-grinder?

An important truth lurks here. As Christians, still in this world (John 17:11), we live in furnished accommodation. Our task is to learn to live in Christ within the given furniture. Satan is part of that furniture. To ask for the banishment of Satan is to ask that earth become heaven.

So Timothy said nothing about some great exorcism by which Satan was thrown out of Thessalonica. Neither – please notice it – did he say that their circumstances had changed for the better and that persecution and opposition had died down.

This too is very important. We are not yet at home in heaven, where everything will be ideal and where, as in Eden, the environment will be on the side of holiness (Isaiah 11:6–9) without anything to hurt or destroy (Matthew 13:41). It is not so now. There are any number of things and people that hurt and destroy, and it always will be so on earth. To want it to be otherwise is natural and right; to expect it to be so is impossible within the terms on which we live in our furnished apartments.

What then? Timothy brought back 'good news about your faith and love', about their continuing happy memories of Paul and their 'longing' to see him and his companions (verse 6). Paul found himself 'encouraged about you because of your faith' (verse 7). Timothy had found them 'standing firm in the Lord' (verse 8). When the apostle revealed what he was praying about for them, it was for the 'supply of what is lacking in your faith' (verse 10).

To Paul, all this was like an injection of new life, a matter for inexpressible thanksgiving and a stimulus to 'pray most earnestly' (verse 10). He really was delighted, wasn't he? Plainly he had heard news of top-priority importance. We will look at his priorities in the order he mentions them. Four things, then:

First, Timothy reported that the Thessalonians were faithfully maintaining the Christian virtues of 'faith and love' (verse 6). Christian victory is just going on being a Christian, whatever Satan may do, whatever circumstances may be like. In 1:2 we heard of their work produced by faith and their labour prompted by love. They are the same virtues that still excite Paul: the basic 'bread and butter' of Christian living.

Secondly, then, in Paul's priorities comes continuing in fellowship with himself. They cherished 'pleasant memories'. (Can't you hear them: 'Do you remember when Paul was here …?') They 'longed' to see him as much as he to see them (verse 6). It is an intense word – used, for example, of the homesick Epaphroditus (Philippians 2:26). This must have meant much to Paul, because he seems to have been dogged in his ministry by detractors ready to cast doubts not only on his character and conduct but also on his teaching.

The question for us is how we are to continue in Paul's fellowship – indeed, in the fellowship of the apostles, now that they are all gone and are irreplaceable. The answer is in 2 Timothy. Paul lived to endure the sadness of people deserting him (1:15), denying central truth (2:18), breaking the Christian moral code (3:1–5) and offering alternative gospels (4:3–4). Timothy's reaction to this was to hold on to apostolic *teaching* (1:13–14; 3:10, 14), to work at and continue with the word of God (2:15; 3:15–17; 4:2). Apostolic *persons* are gone; apostolic *truth* remains. We do not have Paul, but we do have the Bible.

Thirdly in his priorities Paul notes their Christian stability. They are 'standing firm' (verse 8). Putting this another way, they were developing and practising Christian *habits* of thought, word and deed. Trouble was producing endurance (Romans 5:3; James. 1:2–4), and in the best possible sense they were becoming set in their ways. Billy Graham was once charged in a television interview with having a closed mind, but he was easily able to show the silliness of automatically thinking that a closed mind is a bad thing. He replied that he and his wife had been married for a certain number of years and his mind was closed to the possibility of ever being with another woman. Who could deny that just such a closed mind would do a power of good if it were universal today? We need to have the 'closed mind' as our objective in so many, many ways: to become immovably wedded to biblical truth, to biblical moral standards, to biblical lifestyles, to biblical reactions to life's experiences and trials. In other words, we need to become daily more like Jesus, who always did what was pleasing to his Father (John 8:29).

This leads us straight into the *fourth* priority Paul mentions. The Thessalonians kept close to Jesus. They stood firm not through any natural fortitude or personal stickability but through the strength that God supplies. They were 'standing firm in the Lord' (verse 8). Here, as in 1:1 and wherever the same wording is used, 'in' the Lord means 'in close and intimate union' with him. Though their intimate union with the Lord Jesus was something he had granted to them, it was also something they committed themselves to maintain. He set up the relationship; they determined to practise it. Everything, therefore, that kept Jesus clear in their memories, sharp in their minds and determinative for their behaviour was part of their programme – the word of God, the place of prayer, fellow-ship and worship, godly conversation. Daily, as Paul must have envisaged them, they would have been doing what he commanded Timothy to do (1 Timothy 4:9–15).

Questions

1. What is fellowship? How is it expressed? How does it work out? What things bind Christians together? Is it true of our local church? What do we do to enrich local fellowship?
2. On the basis of verse 10, for what was Paul actually praying for the Thessalonians? In what way should these be our concerns for Christians in far-off places? Are we too obsessed with earthly comforts and provisions?
3. The root of the matter is always the Lord Jesus. How can we cultivate a steady and deepening relationship with him so that we are ever more consciously and fully 'in the Lord'? How can we support each other in this?

1 Thessalonians 3:11–13

What to pray for

A striking prayer under the shadow of persecution.

Did you ever see someone's mouth drop open with amazement? Years ago I worked for a Christian organization which found itself under threat of closure. It had been in operation on that site for nearly fifty years without attracting media attention, but with this whiff of crisis we were, of course, inundated with reporters and cameras. Our top man was interviewed on television news.

'And what do you propose to do about all this?' asked the interviewer.

'Oh,' was the reply, 'we have organized a day of prayer with fasting.'

The camera returned to the interviewer just in time to see his lower jaw hit his chest. You could see right into his mind: 'These Christians!! Unpractical to the last!'

Was Paul being 'unpractical to the last' when in prayer he ignored the Thessalonians' circumstances, their dangers and their suffering, and asked only for their growth in love (verse 12) and their perfecting in holiness (verse 13)? In other words, there is a Christian priority: growing in the likeness of Christ in love and holiness. Spiritual concerns come first.

How Paul prayed

Since 2:17 Paul has been occupied with his anxieties over the Thessalonians. How are they placed? Are they spiritually on the straight and narrow? Notice how naturally he slips into prayer. Prayer is the simple deflecting of all our situations upwards to God. Christians should be like mirrors, angled so that whatever meets them on their earthly way is at once – almost without having to think about it – sent up to their heavenly Father. This is not, of course, to say that we don't need disciplined times of prayer, intercession and thanksgiving. But we should (as a friend once said) be always 'found nattering to the Lord'.

On the proper page of my school atlas (page 1, of course!) was a map of my homeland, Ireland. But a little further in, on the same sized page, was a map of Australia. In the corner of the Australia page was a tiny Ireland, no bigger than a child's thumbnail, labelled 'Ireland on the same scale'. Of course, the editor could have done it the other way. He could have attached to the Ireland page a map of Australia, opening out fold upon fold, and entitled 'Australia on the same scale'. That is precisely what praying

Paul-style (Bible-style) does. Alongside ourselves, our situation, our needs, our problems, it opens up, fold upon fold, another picture: 'God on the same scale'. How great, lovely and wonderful he is! How tiny we and our problems! Tiny but not insignificant – simply overshadowed protectively, caringly and sufficiently by the hugeness of our God.

Paul's prayer is full of the work of God and, by implication, of our dependence on what he alone can do. History itself, circumstances and individual persons are all alike under his hand. As to history, when the time comes according to his will, the Lord Jesus will return and the history of the cosmos will be wound up (verse 13). As to circumstances, Paul is dependent on God to open his way back to Thessalonica (verse 11). Not only the great climactic event of the second coming, but the tiny event of getting from Athens to Thessalonica, are alike his appointments.

In addition, the personal, individual matter of each Christian's development of Christian characteristics (verse 12) and growth in holiness (verse 13) is something he alone can do. Paul spoke of their faith and love in verse 6, and then went on to concentrate on faith (verses 7, 10). This is proper, because faith is the fundamental Christian characteristic. It is where we start (John 1:12; Acts 16:30–31), and 'believers' is the commonest New Testament title for Christians. But love is the foremost Christian attribute, the chief evidence of a true faith.

Paul's prayer now moves from the outward showing of Christlike love to the hidden place of the heart (verse 13), so that it may become 'blameless and holy'. Sanctification starts from the inside (Romans 12:2; Ephesians 4:23) – otherwise the display of love is pretence without root. If we are to be Christlike outwardly in love, we must become Christlike inwardly in holiness of heart. 'Blameless' is really 'unblameable': such a heart that no-one can level an accusation against, and that can stand, without accusation, before the throne of God.

All Paul's longing to return to Thessalonica was frustrated by Satan (2:18). The hostility stirred up in

Thessalonica was Satan's open door to tempt and test (3:5). The remedy is to bring in on our own side him who is stronger than the strong (Luke 11:21–22; 1 John 4:4), and this is done through prayer. It is not by the banishment of Satan that Paul will reach Thessalonica, but by the sovereign will of Father and Son (verse 11).

Paul looks to God to provide for all his needs: both for his own journey (verse 11) and for our growth in spiritual maturity (verses 12–13). Left to our own devices, what could we do to become like Jesus? But notice how emphatically his prayer starts by fixing our eyes on 'our God and Father himself and our Lord Jesus' (verse 11). The verb 'clear the way' is singular in the Greek, and binds these two divine Persons into a unity. They are alike on our side, as the repeated possessive pronoun 'our' shows. All this power is 'for us' (Romans 8:31, 37) and the place of prayer is the place of power.

Questions

1. Compose a biblical prayer, related to some need in your church at the moment, or to some friend under pressure, or to some Christians in a land where they are in want and subject to persecution.
2. Read 1 Thessalonians 3:1–10. What truths and thoughts does it prompt which turn into praise and prayer? (Or take Psalm 23, or Isaiah 6:1–8, or some passage of your own choice.)
3. How can we promote love in the fellowship and holiness in each other?
4. In chapter 4, Paul will return to the topic of the 'coming' of the Lord Jesus. Why do you think he mentions it here (verse 13)? What difference does it, and should it, make to our lives?

Bible prayers

How many prayers have you heard beginning, 'O Lord, we thank you …'? And sadly, very often, people who are leading in prayer in public then pause because they haven't planned what they want to thank the Lord for! But look at those first three words: 'O Lord, *we* …' Bible prayers are quite different; they typically begin, 'O Lord, *you* …' They begin by telling God about God. In this way they allow what is true about God to lead into appropriate praise, thanksgiving and prayer.

Look at the prayer in Acts 4:24–30. In my Bible it takes up sixteen lines of print, and of these spends nearly thirteen lines telling God what he is like. The actual request seems almost to come as an 'Oh, by the way …' afterthought! Very different from the way we rush to request! In the Acts 4 prayer, God is seen as Creator (verse 24), speaking in Scripture (verse 25a), sovereign over the nations (verses 25b–26) and presiding over those gathered in Jerusalem at the time of the death of the Lord Jesus so that they did what he willed (verses 27–28). In the light of this reality of managerial power, all they then need to do in relation to those who threaten them is to ask the Lord to 'consider their threats'. Do you see how their theology of the greatness of God puts their problem in perspective?

In the light of this pattern – (a) telling God about God; (b) asking God about us – look at the prayers in Nehemiah 9, Daniel 9 and Psalm 86 (no request till verse 11; no mention of the problem till verse 14).

Every day George Müller of Bristol used to kneel with his Bible open, reading the word of God and turning what he read into adoration, thanksgiving and intercession, and allowing the revealed truth of God to guide his human words in the presence of God. This is a real antidote to the unthinking and self-centred 'O Lord, we' type of prayer. It also has the related advantage of praying the word of God, thoughtfully and meditatively, into our minds and hearts.

Holiness

Apart from the references to the Holy Spirit in 1:5–6, this passage has mentioned 'holiness' for the first time in 1 Thessalonians. What is 'holiness'?

We have to go far back in the Old Testament for a starting-point. Genesis 38:12–28 is one of the cleverest short stories ever told – a real puncturing of pomposity! The widowed Judah was away from home sheep-shearing, saw a girl he fancied and, for an agreed price, spent the night with her. He sent a friend the following day with the payment, and, when he came to the place, he asked (not for the address of the local prostitute but), 'Where is the holy girl ...?' (Genesis 38:21, literally).

Holy? Yes, in the sense that 'holiness' means 'separated-ness', belonging to a different sphere of life. However strange it seems to us, the Canaanite god Baal was worshipped by sexual rites, and both women and men gave themselves in devotion to this god in this way, 'separating' themselves to belong to the god's sphere of life. So they were called 'holy', meaning distinct, separated, belonging elsewhere.

When the God of the Bible is called 'holy', it still has the same basic meaning. The Lord is distinct, different, separated, uniquely himself. But what makes him distinct? That is the key question. The answer comes in Isaiah 6:1–8. This passage teaches that

▶ His is a moral holiness.

▶ His holiness is what makes him distinct from sinners and separates sinners from him.

▶ His holiness is an active force dangerous to outsiders, automatically distancing them from him, barring approach, condemning them to ruin and loss.

▶ But verses 6–8 shows another side of the divine holiness. It is from the holy God that the seraph flies to bring the means of forgiveness, cleansing and atonement to the sinful prophet. The holy God, who is the judge of sinners, is also their saviour.

When we, then, are called to be holy, what does it mean? It is a call to be like him; a call to be separate, distinct in relation to the world around; and a call to moral perfection. But our holiness is not a reaction against the world: 'Because they do something, we won't do it, and by keeping clear of it we will show our difference.' That is negative. Rather, the holiness we are called to is positive: to be like him. Our holiness is to show itself as we model ourselves on the example of Jesus, and obey his holy word.

1 Thessalonians 4:1–8

God's holy will

What does the Lord want me to do? The answer is, 'To be holy.'

'What are you going to be when you grow up?' adults ask, meaning 'What job or profession do you have in mind?' The Bible is concerned about our jobs, but much more about our holiness. Whether the job is at home or overseas, in teaching, in an office or factory or shop, whatever, wherever – the will of God is our holiness.

The first two and a half verses of this section are concerned with the life that pleases God: with holiness. From the second part of verse 3, Paul concentrates on one aspect of living: sexuality.

This passage is full of the idea of our 'active pursuit' of holiness: we are to 'live' (literally, 'walk', verse 1). The double appeal, 'ask' and 'urge' (verse 1), emphatically addresses our wills. There are 'instructions' to obey (verse 2) and 'God's will' to do (verse 3). The 'control' of the body is something we must achieve; no-one is going to do it for us (verse 4). Also, we must respond to the knowledge of God we uniquely possess (verse 5). There is a divine judgment to avoid (verse 6), a calling to follow (verse 7) and an 'instruction' to observe in the power of the indwelling Spirit (verse 8).

Two very important truths are taught in this way.

First, we can live the life of holiness only through obedience. Romans 6:15–23 is a key passage calling us, who by nature are slaves to sin (verses 16–17), to become slaves to obedience (verse 16), to righteousness (verse 18) and to God (verse 22). It promises that slavery to righteousness leads to holiness (verse 19).

Related to this important truth is a *second*. Our work for holiness is effective only because of the completeness of God's work in us. Because the Lord is achieving our holiness, we must do the same. It is his inward work that makes our outward, responsive work possible and worthwhile.

This work of holiness is a work of *obeying God*. Paul refers here (verse 1) to authoritative tradition: 'we instructed you' paraphrases 'you received from us'. We met this verb 'to receive' in 2:13. It means accepting what has been reliably handed down, in this case handed down through the apostles from the Lord (Hebrews 2:3–4) – authoritative apostolic tradition. This is reinforced by the rest of the passage.

Verse 2: 'instructions' are authoritative apostolic commands. As Christians we are 'under authority' (Matthew

8:9) – for how can we possibly know how to 'walk' and 'please God' (verse 1) unless he reveals his requirements to us?

Verse 3: 'it is God's will that you should be holy'. Paul means 'God's revealed will', what he has let us know will please him.

Verse 4: Paul's meaning is a little uncertain, but clearly he is putting holiness into the practical area of sexual purity and self-discipline.

Verse 5: it is implied that if only the heathen 'knew God', they would not behave as they do. In other words, the knowledge of God that he has revealed to us includes the way he wants us to live.

Verse 6: Paul speaks of having 'warned' the Thessalonians about conduct that invites divine judgment.

Verse 7: God's call includes avoiding impurity and pursuing holiness.

Verse 8: the word 'instruction' has been helpfully added by NIV in order to make the meaning clear. Paul said simply 'he who rejects does not reject man but God', but plainly he is looking back over the whole passage. Its 'instruction' about apostolic teaching, knowledge of God, the will of God, the call of God and the judgment of God all in one way or another emphasizes that we are not left on our own to try to sort out what the good life might be. The way we are to live has been revealed in the same way as what we are to believe. God has spoken.

Questions

1. How does this passage teach or imply that we can promote our own holiness?
2. It is not easy today to accept the church's authority about how we should live (verse 1). How far have the church and its leaders the right to tell us how to live? How far are we free to follow the Bible according to our own understanding?
3. Like Paul, we live in an age of great confusion about sex.

Increasingly, all sorts of sexual practices are being accepted as normal. What can we do, as churches, to promote sexual holiness among ourselves and in society around us?

1 Thessalonians 4:3b–8

Avoid sexual immorality

We are all called to control our appetites and passions.

Paul has one particular matter of obedience to raise with his Thessalonians: to 'avoid sexual immorality'. The word very broadly covers the whole area of sexual misbehaviour. It was particularly stressed by the Council of Jerusalem (Acts 15:20, 29; 21:25). Isn't sex as important an area of Christian separation and distinctiveness now as ever it was in Paul's day? Maybe the only difference between the two periods is that in Paul's time sex was often a part of religious observance (as in the worship of Aphrodite), while today it is almost a religion in its own right. It must, of course, have been an area of particular temptation in Thessalonica for Paul to bring it into such prominence here; but if he were writing to us, his modern-day Thessalonians, would he say any different?

Paul is very practical in his teaching about Christians and sex. He takes us through six aspects of the topic.

First, *holiness* (verse 4). The body in its sexual powers is designed for holiness. Remember that 'control' means 'bring to fulfilment'. It is the world's way to see indulgence as fulfilment, and to resent restrictions as a denial of proper development. Not so, says the apostle (and the Bible). Since we have been created in the image of God (Genesis 1:26–27), it is by living in accordance with that image (*i.e.* in holiness) that we come to maturity and a fulfilling life.

Second, *distinctness* (verse 5). Sex is one of the most obvious ways in which we are to stand out from the world. But this is not to be a 'reactive distinctness' ('Because they do it, we won't'), but a 'responsive distinctness', responding to the knowledge of God which we have and they do not. In fact, living according to the word of God (where else do we find the knowledge of God?) is the way of proper 'separation' from the world.

Third, *fellowship* (verse 6a). The church, as a community of the family of God, is to be marked by sexual purity, and in particular by a total respect for the inviolability of Christian marriage. If a woman is a Christian's wife she is out of bounds; likewise if a man is a Christian's husband.

Fourth, *fear* (verse 6b). We must never lose sight of the wrath of a holy God. Paul was so serious about this that he made it part of his initial basic teaching to the infant church. He does not need now to elaborate what he had, 'already told' and affirmed to them. This is not a reference to eternal punishment – though sexual sins are a stated factor in that too (Ephesians 5:3–6; 1 Corinthians 6:9; Revelation 21:8) – but to the discipline of the heavenly Father within his family (Hebrews 12:1–10).

Fifth, *vocation* (verse 7). We have already noted that the 'call' of God is his authoritative 'conscription' of us. Like the true sovereign that he is, he has declared that we are not what we once were. He has put us in a new situation, given us a new status and imposed new requirements matching our new position. Think of someone who was once a civilian, but now, by government diktat, is a soldier (however much he or she still has to learn about soldiering). This person was once a free agent, but is now under orders. Similarly, we were once darkness, but are now light (Ephesians 5:8). Our calling is not impurity but holiness, *i.e.* to be conformed to the divine image (Ephesians 4:23–24).

Sixth, *enabling* (verse 8). This passage began (verses 1–2) with Christians under the word of God to direct them in the life of a holy sexuality; it ends with Christians indwelt by the Holy Spirit to enable them to live that life. To turn from the word of God is to turn from the God who, by his gift of the Holy One, makes holy living possible.

Questions

1. Taking 3:11–13 and 4:1–8, what do we learn about Father, Son and Holy Spirit?
2. We are to be distinct from 'the heathen' (verse 5; compare Ephesians 4:17–24). Why? Where should the difference show? How is the difference achieved? Who are 'the heathen' today?
3. Has your church set up suitable ways of marriage instruction, marriage preparation and marriage rescue? What would be helpful?

Marriage and sex

That sounds the wrong way round, doesn't it? Shouldn't we put it the usual way round and say 'Sex and marriage'? Many books on the subject start with 'growing up', move on to the facts about sex, advance to 'friendships', on to 'courtship' and finally get round to marriage. Should we follow them? No! The Bible, indeed, has little to say about engagement. It suggests that the important thing is to understand about marriage and let that settle every other question – what we think about sex, how we behave in courtship and engagement.

At Genesis 2:4 we move into the beginnings of the human story, and consequently the majestic transcendence of the God who 'speaks and it is done' (Genesis 1:1 – 2:3) is exchanged for the revelation of the LORD God who kindly associates himself with human life and welfare. Thus the

Creator allows himself to be pictured (Genesis 2:18) as if suddenly surprised that all is not well with his favoured creation, humankind. The man is 'alone' and that is 'not good'! Something must be done about it!

What the Lord God does *not* do is almost as significant as what he *does*. He does not say, 'Well, Adam has all those animals. Let him be satisfied with the companionship of a dog.' Nor does he proceed to create another man – even though true male friendship is a very precious thing. The 'good' for man is one who is 'bone of my bones and flesh of my flesh' (verse 23), the female 'matching counterpart' (this is what 'suitable', verse 18, means). In the Hebrew of verse 23, 'man' sounds like *'eesh'*, and 'woman' is the corresponding feminine form, sounding like *'eeshah'*. They are the matching pair, complete only in their togetherness.

The remarkable story of the formation of the woman depicts this relationship. In taking part of the man's body, the Lord God left the man incomplete. When he brought the woman to him, he was bringing back that which would restore the completeness that had been lost. In the same way, the separate part was isolated, away from its proper place; the woman coming to the man is coming home, back to where she belongs. She was taken, says an old commentator, not from his foot, for him to tread on, nor from his head to lord it over him, but from his side and next to his heart. This is what lies behind the thought of the married couple becoming 'one flesh' (verse 24): the lost wholeness is recovered.

This new relationship is primary and exclusive. It takes precedence over existing relationships (however important) to such an extent that the Bible says the man must 'leave his father and mother'. This does not, of course, mean 'leave them in the lurch', and to cease to show them love, care, responsibility and honour; but it does mean that the old relationship has been replaced and superseded by this new relationship in which he 'cleaves to his wife' (verse 24). The verb means 'stick hard', like that glue that creates a permanent and unbreakable bond.

In the creation of this new 'one-flesh' unity, sexual

intercourse is primary and all-important. Engaged couples can talk together, pray together and hold each other in loving embrace, but the one thing they must not do is have sexual intercourse. That is for marriage; indeed, that *is* marriage. It is the act in this on-going relationship that constitutes, nourishes, promotes and seals the one-flesh unity, and does so in the context of life-long commitment, daily mutual care, comfort and support and (usually but not essentially) the procreation and nurture of children. However startling this may seem in our modern world, the Bible could not be clearer on the point.

The Bible opposes casual sex and homosexual conduct, and both for the same reason: they are not consistent with its doctrine of marriage. Casual relationships, indeed any relationships that come short of the total, lifelong commitment of formal marriage, fail to consent to and achieve the ideal of the one-flesh unity. In homosexual or lesbian intercourse, neither partner is finding that which brings completeness, only that which shares and intensifies incompleteness.

Important references for further study: Genesis 2:18–25; Exodus 20:14; 22:16–19; Leviticus 18:1–20; 20:10–26; Matthew 19:1–9; Mark 10:1–12; Acts 15:20; Romans 1:24–32; 1 Corinthians 6:9–11, 12–20; 7:1–40; Galatians 5:19; Ephesians 5:3–6, 21–33; Colossians 3:5–6; 1 Timothy 4:3; Hebrews 13:4; 1 Peter 3:1–7.

4

CHRISTIAN RESPONSIBILITIES

1 Thessalonians 4:9 – 5:11

Stop and look: caring for each other

Part 4's 'banner headlines' tell us what the next sections of 1 Thessalonians are all about:

- ▶ 'About brotherly love' (4:9)
- ▶ 'About those who fall asleep' (4:13)
- ▶ 'About times and dates' (5:1).

Each of these headline topics brings a responsibility. Brotherly love (4:9) brings the responsibility to 'love each other' (4:9) – and not just the immediate Christian family but 'all the brothers throughout Macedonia'; and to love them with a love that is always greater and wider tomorrow than it was yesterday: 'to do so more and more'.

Knowing the truth about Christians *who fall asleep*, that is, who die, brings the responsibility to 'encourage each other' (4:18) with these truths – that they are safe with Jesus and will come with him when he comes (verse 14) and that we will all then be together again, *with the Lord* (verse 17).

Since the plainest truth 'about times and dates' (5:1) is that we do not know the time or date (5:2), then in relation to this certain but unknown event we have a duty to 'encourage one another and build each other up' so that we are all alike confident and well prepared for his return (5:11).

Now notice another way in which these three headlined paragraphs link together. The section on brotherly love ends with a glance *outwards* at the watching world, to 'win the respect of outsiders' (4:12).

Paul's teaching about 'those who fall asleep' ends with a call for a sustained watchfulness *inward*, within the church, so as to share the truth with one another and bring encouragement where it is needed in the fellowship (4:18).

When he reminds us that the surest thing we know about the time of the coming is that we do not know, he is calling us to a *forward* look, to make sure that we are in the highest state of preparedness for our returning Lord (5:10), as indeed his concluding prayer actually says: 'that your whole spirit, soul and body be kept blameless at the coming of our Lord' – a tall order indeed! But we are not alone: 'The one who calls you is faithful and he will do it' (verse 24).

1 Thessalonians 4:9–12

Loving one another

Far from wronging each other (verse 6), we should rather cherish 'brotherly love'.

Here is an interesting statistic. In Romans, Paul addresses his readers as 'brothers' nine times in sixteen chapters, or once in every forty-eight verses. In 1 Corinthians he uses 'brothers' twenty times in sixteen chapters, or once in every twenty-two verses. In 1 Thessalonians he calls them 'brothers' thirteen times in five chapters, or once in every seven verses! There was something very special between Paul and his Thessalonians (2:17; 3:1, 5, 9–10), and he calls them to have this same love for each other.

Of course, 'brothers' sounds unacceptably 'male' to us. We need to take account of two things. First, Paul was equally appreciative of and concerned about Christian 'sisters' (Romans 16:1, 15; 1 Timothy 5:2; Philippians 4:2–3; Philemon 2); and secondly, just as in Hebrews 11:23, where the Greek says 'fathers' and NIV rightly translates the word as 'parents', so we may assume that, for example, in John 2:12 'brothers' includes sisters and means 'family'. The heart of the matter is that we are all bound together in the closest family bonds, and this is to be expressed in mutual love.

This is a way of life God has revealed for his children. Paul says that he does not need to write about it, because 'you yourselves have been taught by God' (verse 9). But, of course, he does go on to write about it, because it is his duty to bring the word of God to bear on his readers.

'Taught by God' (verse 9) is a single Greek word, possibly invented by Paul himself. How does God teach us to love? In two ways.

Lydia (Acts 16:15) and the jailer (Acts 16:33) are beautiful examples of the first way: an *immediate intuition of love* rising in the newly converted heart. At conversion, by the Holy Spirit, Father and Son come to live in our hearts (John 14:17, 23). The Holy Trinity is the eternal family of love, and love is therefore foremost in the new nature of the believer.

God also teaches us *in his Word* to be loving. The new nature inside, and the word outside, speak the same language. The Lord Jesus commanded us to love one another as the primary mark of being his disciples (John 13:34–35; 15:12, 17). The Scriptures repeat the command (1 John 2:7–11; 3:11). James blends intuition and obedience together when he commands us to 'accept the word planted in you' (1:21). The implanted word is our new nature in Christ, the new heart with the word of God inscribed on it (Jeremiah 31:31–34; Hebrews 10:15–18); our 'accepting' the word is our conscious obedience to what the word of God says.

How happy Paul must have been to see his Thessalonians busy in this double task of living out their new nature and obeying God's word. They were already living like that: 'you do love'. They were also spreading their love to all Christians around: 'all the brothers'. Yet Paul was avid for more: 'do so more and more'. Since the God who dwells in our hearts is Love (1 John 4:8), and since our Lord Jesus commanded love (John 13: 34), surely we can't have enough of it!

We now come to a most interesting question. In verses 11–12 Paul urges a threefold lifestyle:

▶ to lead a quiet life

▶ to mind your own business, and

▶ to work with your hands.

His readers are to do all this 'so that' two results will follow: they will

▶ win the respect of outsiders, and

▶ not be dependent.

I say that he 'urges' all this, because in the Greek of his letter what we call verse 11 follows directly on 'We urge you' in verse 10, so that it could be translated, 'We urge you to do so more and more and to make it your ambition.' The threefold lifestyle is not three separate commands but three distinct ways in which the 'more and more' of verse 10 will work out.

Look at it this way. The obligation to love the family of God and to do so ever more and more could easily lead to a frenzy of activity, duties to other Christians becoming a burdensome mountain of obligations. Don't let your life become like that: 'Make it your ambition to lead a quiet life.'

Again, the exercise of brotherly love – a deepening concern for the true welfare of others – could lead to undue and unwelcome poking our noses into other people's lives, offering gratuitous advice – 'You know I am only saying/doing/suggesting this out of love.' Rather, 'mind your own business', make yourself your first port of call.

Some people understood the command of brotherly love to mean that everyone else had an obligation to keep *them* in the style to which they thought themselves entitled (2 Thessalonians 3:6–12). No, brotherly love does not allow us to freeload, to sponge. Rather, 'work with your [own] hands', let your own efforts provide for your own needs.

At any rate, Christians (Paul 'urges' in verses 10–11) should be noted for

▶ their *peacefulness* – 'lead a quiet life'.

▶ a *proper reserve*, a holding back from anything which could be criticized as wanting to run other people's lives.

▶ a *practical self-reliance*: Paul, of course, is not requiring every Christian to undertake manual work as such, but to make one's own efforts meet one's own needs – an efficient work ethic.

This is the lifestyle that wins respect from the watching world (verse 12).

In a homegroup in our church a questioner asked, 'What would really command the attention of the watching world today?'

The voice of a woman who only occasionally contributed piped up: 'Peace,' she said.

Everyone rounded on her. 'Come on, Margaret, tell us more!'

'Well,' she said, 'I live in a apartment block of twelve flats. In most of them there is some sort of trouble, small and great – all are under pressure. What they need more than anything else is to see people who live in the same troubled world, meet the same difficulties and still enjoy an unflurried peace.'

That is exactly what Paul meant.

There is no need to explain the other two matters further. Poking our noses into other people's business is no testimony, whether it is over-interference, or bossiness on the part of church leaders, or insensitive prying into people's privacy ('I'm only asking so that I can pray about it!'). And idleness! (Of course, Paul is speaking of sponging as a way of life, not the enforced idleness of illness, age or unemployment.) It speaks for itself.

Questions

1. Is your church a loving fellowship? How can we increase loving care among believers and keep the balance between concern and non-interference? Or unobtrusively make money available to those who are short? What new ways are there to extend brotherly love more and more?
2. What, in fact, is Christian love? How can we in a proper sense 'keep ourselves to ourselves' and at the same time keep open house to the needy?
3. How do we cultivate a peaceful and unflurried lifestyle when life is so bothersome and, with the best will in the world, it is so easy to become over-busy?

1 Thessalonians 4:13–15

What about those who have died?

We can be sure that those who have died in Christ are alive in Christ.

Paul has a formula for solving problems. People have got something wrong, and in the most loving way he says, 'Brothers, we do not want you to be ignorant.' Look up Romans 1:13; 1 Corinthians 10:1; 12:1; 2 Corinthians 1:8.

We can put their problem this way. The Lord Jesus is returning soon. So what about Christians who even now are dying (notice the present tense in verse 13, meaning 'those

who are falling asleep') and will miss out on the great
event?

What Jesus taught

Paul turns first to 'the Lord's own word' (verse 15). Jesus
told his disciples about his coming again. He taught that he
will come from heaven (Matthew 24:30; compare verse 16 of
our passage), with clouds (Mark 13:26; verse 17) and with a
trumpet blast (Matthew 24:31; verse 16) to gather his people
to himself (Matthew 24:31; verse 17). He also taught us to
cultivate urgent watchfulness (Matthew 24:39, 42, 44, 50;
25:13) for this certain but undated event.

Coming soon?

They were not wrong, therefore, to be absorbed with the
thought of a soon-coming Lord, even though it gave them a
problem about friends who were dying. We, of course,
know that two thousand years have gone by, and it would
be as mistaken as it is easy to jump to the conclusion that
Paul's imminent expectation has been proved wrong.
Rather, we should say that he lived in daily expectation *and
was right to do so, because this is what Jesus taught*. Paul knew
that the great event was undateable (5:1), and he would
never have said any such thing as, 'Jesus is sure to come
before I die.' His reference to 'we who are still alive' (verse
17) expresses longing that he should be alive, but not
affirmation that he will be. As long as this life lasts, we are
all called to live in imminent hope of the Lord's return.

Death

Verse 13a speaks of 'those who fall asleep'. Jesus got himself
laughed at when he went into the bedroom of Jairus'
twelve-year-old daughter and, in the face of 'expert
opinion', pronounced her 'not dead but asleep' (Luke 8:52).
Had she not died, then? Oh yes! The experts laughed,
'knowing that she was dead' (Luke 8:53). The point is that

they were both right. To them she was dead, gone beyond that point of no return; to him, she was asleep (John 11:11–15). He brought into the situation those other dimensions in which he lived and those other powers he possessed. To him, death is sleep, and recalling a girl from death is a matter of pressing a little hand and speaking a gentle word (Luke 8:54), just like a father waking his sleeping daughter for breakfast.

Grief

Paul does not tell us (in verse 13b) that we shouldn't grieve. This often troubles bereaved Christians: they feel that to give way to tears is being less than 'triumphant', too subject to earthly perspectives and present infirmities. It is not so. When we are 'in Christ' everything is new (2 Corinthians 5:17).

> Heaven above is softer blue; earth around is
> sweeter green:
> Something lives in every hue Christless eyes have
> never seen.

And our emotions too are 'new', sharper than before, more sensitive. Far from being 'triumphant', we feel sorrow more keenly; tears come more readily. Had Epaphroditus died, Paul said he would have experienced 'sorrow upon sorrow' (Philippians 2:27) – the same Paul who said of his own death that it would be 'better by far' (Philippians 1:23)! And why shouldn't Christians weep, when Jesus did (John 11:35)?

Christian grief is not only more sharply felt, but it is also filled with a hope 'the rest' do not have (verses 13c–15). Restore the opening 'For' to the beginning of verse 14: our grief is not like those without hope, *for* 'Jesus died and rose' and 'God will bring with Jesus those who have fallen asleep in [literally "through"] him'.

There are three wonderful truths here.

First, the Lord Jesus presides over our death – the timing

of it, the manner of it, the circumstances in which it occurs. It is too important a matter to leave to anyone else: we die 'through Jesus'.

Secondly, we die in the full security of his finished work of salvation: he 'died and rose'. His death and resurrection *are* the gospel (1 Corinthians 15:1, 3–4). He bore our sins (Isaiah 53:4–6,10–12; 1 Peter 2:22–25) and satisfied the holy wrath of God (Romans 3:24–25, 'sacrifice of atonement', literally, 'propitiation', the satisfying and taking away of God's just anger). For all eternity he has settled the problem of our sin, paid our debt, borne our punishment and opened the gate of glory.

Thirdly, those who have died in Christ are in his keeping and will come again with him. The Lord Jesus assured the dying thief who turned to him that 'today you will be with me in paradise' (Luke 23:43; Isaiah 45:22). Paul spoke of death as 'to depart and be with Christ' (Philippians 1:23). There we remain, in his presence and care until the day comes appointed by the Father (Mark 13:32). When that day comes the returning Lord Jesus will bring with him (1 Thessalonians 3:13) those who, since their earthly death, have been with him, which is by far the best (Philippians 1:23).

Hope

Paul uses the great word 'hope' of all this. When we ordinarily speak of hope, we imply a lack of certainty: we 'hope' it will be fine tomorrow, that this or that peace initiative will succeed, or that next year's work will be easier than this year's. But we can't be sure. When the Bible speaks of hope, there is nothing uncertain except the date of fulfilment. The thing hoped for is completely assured. The great certainty in verse 14 is that 'God will bring with Jesus those who have fallen asleep'. There is no greater guarantor.

In this way Paul answers the loving concerns of the Thessalonians. Their dear dead will not be at any disadvantage (verse 15) when Jesus comes again.

Questions

---

1. It is natural to want to pray for our friends and relations who have died. Is there any need? What would we ask? What are the rights and wrongs of praying for the dead?
2. What are the best ways of helping a bereaved Christian? What expectations do we have of how we should 'cope' with bereavement? How are they different from those of an unbeliever?
3. 'Pie in the sky when you die,' say the cynics. What can we say to the world about our hope of life after death?

1 Thessalonians 4:16–18

Listening for the trumpet

We face the future not knowing everything, but knowing enough to be going on with. And what we do know is the most wonderful hope there ever was.

The return (verse 16)

Jesus spoke of his coming again in personal, visible and heavenly terms (Matthew 24:30–31; Mark 13:26–27; Luke 21:27–28); so did the 'men in white' at his ascension (Acts 1:11). Jesus also emphasized that the event would be as unmissable as lightning flashing over the whole sky (Matthew 24:27; Luke 17:24). What an event it will be! Paul does not mention the lightning, but he holds the same view: the return will not happen in secret but will be hugely publicized

▶ by a loud command

▶ by the voice of the archangel, and

▶ by the trumpet of God.

No doubt the Thessalonians knew what these three meant, from Paul's teaching while he was with them. He does not explain them for us – and we can only guess.

Who will give the command? The Lord Jesus said that only the Father knows the day and hour (Mark 13:32; Acts 1:7). Who else then can give the command which sets the great Day in motion? The Father spoke at his Son's baptism (Mark 1:11) and at his transfiguration (Mark 9:7); he spoke in validation of the cross (John 12:27–29). Will he not announce his Son when he comes in glory?

What will the archangel say? The only archangel we know of is Michael.

▶ In Revelation 12:7 he is the victor with his angels over the dragon and his angels.

▶ In Daniel 10:13, 21; 12:1 he is the guardian of the Lord's people who stands up on their behalf.

Michael is thus associated with conquest and victory. When Jesus comes again, will Michael act as his herald, announcing cosmically the visible, public triumph of the King of kings and Lord of lords and calling on every knee to bow (Philippians 2:9–11)?

What trumpet is this and what does it mean (Matthew 24:31; 1 Corinthians 15:52)?

▶ It is the Sinai trumpet (Exodus 19:16), announcing that the Lord is here.

▶ It is the Leviticus trumpet (Leviticus 25:9) proclaiming the liberation of the Lord's people from every enslavement and every debt, and their freedom to possess their possessions.

▶ It is – surely above all – Isaiah's trumpet (27:12–13), gathering into one the Lord's worldwide people.

The resurrection (verses 16c–17a)

How can the 'dead in Christ' be said to 'rise' when verse 14 says that, having been with Christ since their death, they will come with him?

When they went to be with Christ they left part of themselves behind, didn't they? Their spirits went to live on with Christ, but there was part of them that experienced the full earthly reality of death. For this reason they are spoken of here not as those who fell asleep, but as 'the dead': their bodies turned to earthly dust. But, by the terms of our creation, we are bodies as well as souls/spirits; the body is no less 'me' than the spirit. Death shatters the God-intended unity of the embodied soul and the ensouled body, but the return of Jesus is the moment when that unity will be restored – the reconstitution of the whole person, the bringing together of the redeemed soul with the resurrection body (Romans 8:23; 1 Corinthians 15:35–38, 42–54; Philippians 3:20–21; 1 John 3:2).

But if we do not 'precede' them in enjoying the coming, neither do they exceed us in the benefits the returning Lord brings, for 'we who are still alive will be caught up together with them'.

The meeting (verse 17b)

The Lord Jesus is himself the central reality and glory. Everything else will pale into insignificance – recognizing and meeting our 'top ten' of biblical characters, reunion with our best beloved of earthly days, the wonder of our resurrection bodies – nothing will compare with the beauty of Jesus. *He* will be there at the centre of angels and archangels and the whole company of heaven, all the redeemed from every tribe and tongue and people and nation (Revelation 7:9). He will at last unroll the scroll whose seals he alone was worthy to open (Revelation 5); he will call the roll of those whose names are written there, those whom he died to save – and not one will be missing.

But this meeting will take place 'in the clouds ... in the air'. This is to be taken literally: we will really, actually, truly be 'caught up', snatched away from earth, up, to meet him. Beyond this primary, literal meaning there may be a symbolical meaning too.

▶ The clouds speak of the presence of God (Exodus 13:21; Matthew 17:5). At his return the clouds proclaim that Jesus is God, and our reception into the clouds fulfils the fact that Christ died to bring us to God (1 Peter 3:17).

▶ The 'air' is symbolically the domain of Satan (Ephesians 2:2), but at that day it will be the place of dominion of the King of kings, and Satan will at last be bruised under our feet (Romans 16:20).

Eternal security (verse 17c)

The little word 'so' must not be missed. It means 'in this way' – as those who have been fully redeemed in body and soul, those caught up to be with Jesus, those welcomed into the presence of God and freed from the presence of evil. In that blissful state of wholeness, 'we will be with the Lord for ever' (John 14:1–3; 17:24).

Is it any wonder that Paul sees these marvellous truths as the means of our personal and mutual encouragement (verse 18)?

Questions

1. Paul's main teaching about the resurrection body is in 1 Corinthians 15:35–54 and Philippians 3:20–21. This has to be taken into account if we are fully to appreciate what Thessalonians teaches. What then is the resurrection body? What will we be like?

2. How would you answer someone who insisted that in this scientific age we cannot possibly believe in a visibly coming Jesus or in our rising to meet him?
3. How can we keep alive our sense of expectancy and our desire to be pleasing to him when he comes?

1 Thessalonians 5:1–3

Waiting for the day

We do not know *when* he is coming, but we do know *that* he is coming.

Look back. The truth of the second coming of the Lord Jesus rings throughout 1 Thessalonians. Let us remind ourselves of what has been said.

▶ The return of our Lord Jesus Christ makes us *durable*. In all the circumstances of life we hold on in hope (1:3).

▶ The second coming is a basic Christian doctrine. It belongs with the great truths about the one God and his Son, the resurrection and the work of Jesus in providing our eternal security (1:9–10).

▶ It is a day of gathering together and of bringing to him the fruits of our labour (2:19).

▶ God himself is preparing us in holiness for that day (3:13).

▶ The climax. It is the day when we experience salvation in all its fullness (4:13–18).

Do you see that 1 Thessalonians is very truly a letter of hope? From the beginning, to the climax of 4:13–18, Paul has kept coming back to the hope of Christ's return. Now, as he draws his letter to an end, he wants to tell us one final and most important thing: how we prepare.

There was one matter on which Paul had no need to write (verse 1). They already knew it, but maybe they were getting into a tangle about 'times and dates'. People often do. In 1969 I had a letter from a Christian friend informing me that the world would end in 1971. I did not, however, get a letter of repentance and apology in 1972! The Lord Jesus himself does not know the date; it is the Father's secret (Mark 13:32). How foolish of us to probe into 'times' (the calendar date of an event) or 'dates' (the sort of period in which it might happen)! The one thing we know is that we don't know and cannot know. But there is so much we do know, and it is intended to prompt us to a life of readiness.

Inescapable disaster

Paul uses two pictures: the burglar (verse 2) and the pregnant woman (verse 3). Sometimes in the Bible, pregnancy and birth are pictures of joy to come (John 16:21). But not so here. The burglar is a picture of unexpectedness. Outside factors are at work: the burglar planning, deciding, bringing hurt and loss. The pregnant woman is here a picture of inevitability: factors are at work internally in people and the world which must come to this conclusion, and it cannot be escaped.

Between these two pictures Paul sets out the facts: the world, seeing nothing but 'peace and safety', will be as complacent as in the days of Noah: people getting married, men at work, women at household chores (Matthew 24:37–42), when the external factors of God's judgment and the internal factors of human sin will bring 'destruction' without 'escape'.

The particular sin in mind is complacency. The first sin (Genesis 3:4) was the denial of the judgment of God; the final sin is to say 'Peace and safety', refusing the warning of what is to come, namely 'destruction'. This is a word which one writer defines as 'not destruction of being but of well-being, not putting an end to the existence of a person but its ruin so far as the purpose of its existence is concerned'. 'Loss of that life which is life indeed', says another. Paul will say more about this in 2 Thessalonians 1:7–10.

Questions

1. How would you live today if you knew that Jesus would return tomorrow? What changes would you make to your plans? Why? Do you know that he will not return tomorrow?
2. How can we keep a proper balance between concentrating on the second coming too much (scaremongering) and not enough (complacency)?
3. Why is it a sin to say 'Peace and safety'? How far should we work for social and world peace?

1 Thessalonians 5:4–8

We are not in darkness

We know he will come again. So what are we going to do about it?

The second coming will be a day of destruction (verse 3) but also of fulfilment (verses 4–5). We will understand this if we study the important terms that are used.

Darkness is a picture of an estrangement from God (Matthew 4:16; 8:12); of divine judgment, (Matthew 27:45; Exodus 10:21); of the presence and activity of Satan (Luke 22:53); of humankind's natural state (John 3:19; Romans 13:12) and of eternal punishment (Jude 13).

Light pictures that which dispels the darkness (Matthew 4:16; Luke 1:79). Conversion is coming out of darkness into light (2 Corinthians 4:6). Christians are 'sons of light', (Ephesians 5:8). 'Sons of', or sometimes 'children of', is a way of describing the condition in which people are. Those under and deserving God's wrath are 'children of wrath' (Ephesians 2:3).

Putting all this together, what does Paul say about us in these verses?

First, we are not what we once were: 'not in darkness', estranged from God, living out the dark life of our sinful nature and so on.

Second, we possess a new nature ('sons of the light') and live in a new, matching environment ('sons of the day').

Third, neither the 'darkness' (the old, unconverted nature) nor the environment in which it characteristically lives ('the night') has any more ownership-rights over us ('We do not belong to' them).

Fourth, *the day* is coming when we will at last live in our natural environment, totally without any trace or 'pull' of the old darkness. As 'sons of the day', it is our true habitat in which our new nature will come to full flower (Philippians 3:20–21).

So prepare

Notice how verses 6–8 move on from verses 4–5. There, the emphasis was on the *states* of darkness, light, night and day; here the emphasis falls on the *activities* suited to the states. Sleep happens at night; so does drunkenness (verse 7), while wakefulness and alertness (verse 6) and readiness for action (verse 8) are appropriate to the day. Once more the words used are important.

► The verb translated 'be alert' means both to be awake and to be determined to stay awake (Matthew 24:42–43; 25:13; 26:38). To be 'on the alert' catches the meaning exactly.

► *Self-controlled* (verses 6–8) would be better as 'clear-headed', not fuddled or confused, especially keeping our minds and thoughts clear and focused for spiritual things (2 Timothy 4:5; 1 Peter 1:13; 4:7).

► *Sleep*. It is particularly important to be clear about this verb. It is *not* the verb translated 'to sleep' in 4:13, 14 and 15, and it is *never* used as a metaphor for Christian death. It is used of natural sleep (Matthew 8:24; Mark 4:27); it is also used of moral and spiritual carelessness (Ephesians 5:14), and in particular of unalertness in respect of the Lord's return (Matthew 25:5; Mark 13:36). The sleep of the disciples in Gethsemane combines both physical and spiritual meanings (Matthew 26:40, 43, 45).

In preparation for the Lord's coming, then, there are things we must avoid (verses 6–7) and things we must do (verse 8).

▶ We are commanded to avoid anything inconsistent with alert and clear-headed expectation of the coming Lord and which therefore makes us unready (like the sleep of Matthew 25:5) or unfit (like the drunkenness of Luke 12:45) to meet him.

▶ By contrast (verse 8), we are to put on *armour* – that is to say, commit ourselves to the active, battling life of those living each day in waiting for the Day (Romans 13:11–14).

But when Paul speaks of *faith and love as a breastplate, and the hope of salvation as a helmet*, what does he mean? He means this: that it is living the life of *faith*, *love* and *hope* that armour us for whatever each day brings and make us fighting fit in readiness for the day when it comes.

▶ Faith, love and hope are the hallmarks of true Christian living (1:3).

▶ Faith and love are the points at which Christians demonstrate victory over life's adversities (3:6, 8).

▶ Faith, love and hope are our preparedness for the Lord's return (5:8).

Faith points to living with God: trustfully accepting life, with all its varied experiences, as coming to us from him, trustfully leaning upon him to supply our every need and see us through.

Love points to living in warm, reciprocal, caring fellowship with our fellow-Christians and reaching out beyond them to a needy world.

Hope points to living in expectancy: today may be the Day!

Questions

1. What problems do you have with personal discipline? ('I

wish I could …!' 'I wish I hadn't …!') Make a short list. What is there in these verses to help with disciplined living? In the group, share your lists anonymously and discuss the problems raised.

2. In what ways can we set an example of living as children of light as distinct from those who live in darkness? Where does the contrast show? Are there 'grey areas'?

3. The reference to 'armour' (verse 8) suggests we have a fight on our hands. Is this so? Is there any way out of the battle and into peace? Who is the enemy?

1 Thessalonians 5:9–11

What an assurance!

Amid dramatic events and demanding standards, we have the encouragement that God wants us to come through. So be hopeful!

Please remember what we said above about *hope* in the Bible: that it has no 'wishful thinking' in it; it is sure confidence of the fact coupled with ignorance of the time. We do not know when the hoped-for day of completed salvation (verse 8) will come, but come it will, and our salvation itself is absolutely certain. In order that we may grasp this great confidence, Paul adds an explanation set out in four wonderful truths (verses 9–10).

1. *The will of God.* Our salvation does not depend on our determination but on his. 'God did not appoint us to … wrath but to … salvation.' Can his will be defeated or turned aside, or achieve less than he set out to do? Certainly

not (Numbers 23:19)! There is no uncertainty about our destiny: it is 'to possess salvation'.

2. *The Son of God*. Our salvation comes to us 'through our Lord Jesus Christ'. Take each part of his full name and title in turn. He is *Lord* in his full deity (Philippians 2:11; Isaiah 45:22–23), therefore full of power and authority. He is *Jesus* in his humanity, therefore full of sympathy and understanding (Hebrews 4:14–16). He is *Christ*, the one whom the Father 'anointed' to be the Saviour of sinners. He is our salvation.

3. *The cross of Christ*. The Lord Jesus Christ brought all his deity, all his human understanding of our needs and all his power to save to the cross at Calvary. Isaiah (53:11) says that 'by his knowledge' (because he knows exactly what *we* need and *God* requires) 'my righteous servant' (the Lord Jesus in all his perfection: the perfect lamb, Exodus 12:5; the perfect human being, John 19:4) 'provides righteousness' (covers us with his perfections, Romans 3:21–22; 1 Corinthians 1:30; Philippians 3:9).

4. *The guaranteed future*. 'Whether we are awake or asleep, we [will] live with him.' Many think that Paul is here returning to the topic with which he began in 4:13 – what about believers who die before the coming of the Lord? – and that he gives the same reply, rounding off his discussion: that it is of no consequence whether, on that Day, we are alive or asleep (dead). Our salvation cannot ever be in peril; we will live with him.

This, of course, is absolutely true, but is not, I believe, what Paul is saying here. The verb translated 'asleep' is not the one found in 4:13–15 but the one found in 5:6–7. This means that it is *not* the verb used to refer to Christian death but the verb that is *never* used of Christian death: it is used of sleep as a picture of spiritual sloth and unreadiness for the returning Lord. This reference, then, to being 'awake or asleep' brings us to the heart of our eternal security. We are such fluctuating mortals. Today's spiritual keenness becomes tomorrow's spirit of indifference. Nothing is more important today than the Bible; tomorrow we can't be bothered. We are up early today for prayer; tomorrow we're snoring. We are full of testimony today, but tomorrow, silence. And so on and on.

Of course, we always wish it otherwise. As Paul says, in our minds we are slaves to God's law, but in the sinful nature slaves to the law of sin (Romans 7:25). We are proper mixed-up kids. Now, suppose Jesus returned on one of our off days and found us sleeping.

Of course it matters: we would want to die of embarrassment. We would give anything to have that day over again so as to greet him with a shining face, to match our delight in him with his delight in us. But is our salvation in peril? Never (1 Corinthians 3:10–15)! Our salvation depends on the will of God, the Son of God, and the cross of Christ. It is he who chose us, not we him (John 15:16).

Questions

1. Make a list of ways you can encourage other Christians. If you are in a group, share some encouraging things now. Decide how you will put a policy of encouragement into practice.
2. What are the things that make us sleepy and confused as Christians, and how can we cure them?
3. If God is determined on our salvation, why should we bother to live any differently from anyone else?

5

READY FOR CHRIST'S COMING

1 Thessalonians 5:12–28

Stop and look: working for the day

Talk about being light and not darkness, day and not night, awake and not asleep is all very well, but it's a bit vague, isn't it? What actually are we to *do* while we wait for Jesus to return?

What are we to do? We may be sorry we asked when we look at the avalanche of commands in 5:12–22. Paul must have heard us asking!

There are actually fifteen commands, and they look a right old jumble, one thing after another! But actually this is a very carefully composed statement about Christian behaviour. Look at the commands again. They come in five groups of three.

▶ The first three, about life in the church, are 'respect … Hold … Live in peace' (verses 12–13).

▶ Then verse 14 makes a fresh start ('And we urge') with three commands about our relationships ('warn … encourage … help', verse 14b).

▶ Then come three about our characters (patience, non-retaliation and kindness, verses 14c–15).

▶ These are followed by three about spiritual living ('Be joyful … pray … give thanks', verses 16–18).

Notice how these commands start out as something that Paul wants (verse 14, 'we urge you') and end as something that God wants (verse 18, 'God's will for you'): the *apostolic will* (verse 14) and the *divine will* (verse 18). These are therefore no ordinary commands. They are exceedingly important. They tell us how to live as apostolic Christians according to the will of God.

The first of the three final commands touches on the

ministry of the Holy Spirit (verse 19). The second deals with prophecy or hearing God's word (verse 20). The third is to exercise personal spiritual discernment (verse 21a, 'test everything'), which is spelled out as holding on to the good and avoiding the evil (verses 21b–22).

What a very serious list of commandments! We are going to be busy people as we wait for the Lord to come. But in case we get too preoccupied with ourselves and what *we* must do, Paul jogs our elbows with a welcome reminder that when all comes to all, it is *God's* work to make us ready for the coming of his Son (verses 19–23), 'and he will do it' (verse 24).

Just as God's work for our holy readiness in 3:11–13 led into our responsibility to live the holy life (4:1–8), so now our work preparing ourselves for the coming Lord (5:12–22) leads into the complete work of preparation which 'God himself' will do, and do without fail (verses 23–24).

1 Thessalonians 5:12–15

Encouraging one another

In the church we are to live looking up to our leaders (with respect and love) and around to our brothers and sisters (with peace and care).

Leaders in a peaceful community (verses 12–13)

There is no such thing, in the Bible, as a church without leaders, and there is no such thing as a church with a single leader. (Note the condemnation of a 'one-man band' in 3 John 9–11.) Leaders are to be respected for their work. 'Work hard' is the verb linked with the noun translated 'labour' (1:5), 'toil' (2:9) and 'efforts' (3:5). But leaders who display such sacrificial commitment merit *respect* (verse 12). Because they do such work they deserve the 'highest regard' and 'love' (verse 13). Leadership, then, is a function, not a position; an activity, not a status. Paul gives the leadership no distinguishing titles: they are marked out only by *how* they work and *what* they do.

Two aspects of leadership are picked out for special mention. They are 'over you in the Lord' and they 'admonish you'.

The verb translated 'to be over you' means 'to stand before' and so 'to lead, care for, attend to'. In Greek literature it has the technical meaning of 'practising a profession'. Paul carefully qualifies it here by the words 'in the Lord', meaning, not vaguely 'in spiritual matters', but precisely 'in a way that is compatible with their personal union with the Lord', or 'as Jesus himself would have them do' (compare Mark 10:42–45; Luke 22:24–27).

Leaders also 'admonish'. This is in fact a general Christian duty, as the same verb in verse 14 (NIV, 'warn') shows. It is a lovely word, combining tenderness between 'brothers' and firmness in correcting misconduct. Paul exercised this ministry (Acts 20:31), mingling the firmness of his 'warning' about false teachers with his 'tears' of concern for the church.

It is the sort of directive counselling that arises out of goodness of character and concern for the truth (Romans 15:14; 'instruct'). It is the work of a loving parent (1 Corinthians 4:14). It is the product of the word of Christ in the heart (Colossians 3:16), exercised within a worshipping, praising fellowship.

In all this, Paul is speaking to the 'brothers', the whole assembly of church members. They look *up* with respect to those leading; they look *round* with peace towards each other. This is every bit as much a command as anything else in verses 12–13. Peaceful relationships are an obligation; to breach the peace of the church is disobedience to the request of the apostle (verse 12) and to 'God's will' (verse 18).

Mutual ministry (verse 14)

As we would say today, we have to be there for each other. At any moment any one of us might lapse from properly disciplined Christian living. Equally, any of us might fall into low spirits ('timid') or find ourselves 'weak' or despondent in the face of life's demands. Thank God if there is a brother or sister on hand to 'counsel' (the word used in verse 12; 'warn' is much too harsh) with care and sound advice, and to 'encourage' (the word actually means to 'console, condole with', John 11:19, 31), reflecting the comfort of a father when one of his little ones has a tumble (2:12). It is the gentle concern that will not break the bruised reed or stamp out smouldering flax (Isaiah 42:3).

Personal characteristics (verses 14–15)

Notice how all-embracing these three commands are: 'everyone … nobody … always … each other … everyone'. In all our relationships these are to mark us out: patience, non-retaliation, kindness.

Patient is – to make up a word – 'long-tempered', the opposite of 'short-tempered'. Between people, it is perfectly illustrated in Matthew 18:26. It is one of God's characteristics (Luke 18:7, not, as in NIV, 'keep putting them off ', but 'and he is patient with them'; 2 Peter 3:9); it is an aspect of the outworking of love (1 Corinthians 13:4). The noun 'patience' appears as one of the fruits of the Spirit in Galatians 5:22, and it is an aspect of mutual relations among Christians (Ephesians 4:2; Colossians 1:11). In 1:3 Paul praised their 'endurance', which refers to durability under the testings of circumstances; but 'patience' is interpersonal: an unruffled, equable, amenable acceptance of other people whoever they are ('everyone') and however long the pressure lasts.

The second characteristic Paul insists on is that 'nobody pays back wrong for wrong' (verse 15). The appeal 'Make sure' is not a directive (literally) to 'see to it' that everybody else practises the virtue of non-retaliation; it is a command to all for all to obey. 'Paying back' has no place in Christian behaviour. NIV should add 'to anyone' after 'wrong for wrong'. How emphatic then is the command, 'nobody ... to anybody'!

Third, in personal attributes, Paul commands *kindness* (verse 15). The literal translation of what he wrote is emphatic: 'Always keep pursuing the good to one another and to all.' 'The good' of course includes what is morally and spiritually good, what is good in itself, as in verse 21; but it also has the broader meaning of what is 'to the benefit' of a person, the opposite of what hurts or hinders. And, once again, no exceptions are allowed: 'always ... each other ... everyone else'. Notice too the vigour with which this sort of life is to be lived: 'pursue', Philippians 3:12, 14 (NIV, 'press on').

Questions

1. How do you draw the line between being responsible for other Christians ('warn', 'encourage', 'help') and being a busy-body, interfering, bossy? Give examples.
2. In respecting, loving and holding our leaders in high regard, how far do we have to ignore their faults? How best can we support them, and when – if ever – should we speak or act in criticism?
3. How far do these principles of respect for leadership extend to secular organizations?

1 Thessalonians 5:16–18

The joyful will of God

Joyfulness, prayer and thanksgiving are God's will for us all.

Life with God (verses 16–18)

The way the commands are grouped in threes links the joy-command with prayer and thanksgiving. This is then no merely human joy – the breeziness of an extrovert temperament – let alone a pretend-joy, but a joy nourished through bringing all life to God ('pray') and accepting all life from God ('thanks'). At the same time, the joy-command flows out of what has preceded. We would not need to be ordered to be patient or to refuse to retaliate if life were not challenging us along those lines. There are provocations in full and plenty to impatience, and many an opportunity to hit back. In deliberately turning from such things in obedience, it would be easy to develop a stoical dourness and at the same time to become secretly ill-minded ('I know what I would do to you if I weren't a Christian'). Our obedience, on the contrary, is to be full of joy, exercised in prayer and bathed in thanksgiving.

Joy

'Be joyful always' sounds like a pretty pointless command. How can we possibly do it? The problem is that our minds become so preoccupied with our difficulties – very understandably so. When I was a child, earache and toothache were much more common than they seem to be today, and my elders and betters regularly handed out the most pointless remedy humankind ever invented: 'Try not to think about it!' How in the world can one not think about toothache? Yet, even so – even when the ache was sharpest – our small worlds were full of hundreds of other things as well as the pain: good things, happy things. So it is with Christian joy. Whatever the day, whatever the ache, God has not changed, Jesus is the same, salvation is still wonderful, the Bible is at hand, Christian friends are around, the Lord's table is spread, prayer is an open door and the Holy Spirit is the Lord of joy (1:6).

Prayer

Now, as to praying continually (verse 17), think of the way a mirror can reflect a shaft of sunlight and direct it this way and that. When my wife and I visited tombs in the Valley of the Kings, quite often an attendant would sit at the entrance with a large polished sheet of metal directing the Egyptian sunlight into the dark recesses. Our lives should be so angled to God that whatever strikes us is at once reflected up into his presence. I think that when Paul says 'continually' here he is not talking about our regular times set apart for prayer (though not excluding them) but about what a recent letter described as 'consulting Father at leisure about everything', living life constantly on the prayer-level.

Thankfulness

Finally, we 'give thanks in all circumstances', not *for* all circumstances! The latter would not be a totally absurd command, though, because everything that ever comes to us comes from our loving heavenly Father. Even the direst experience is his gift and his will for us – a weed left beside the wheat so that the wheat can come perfect to harvest (Matthew 13:29–30). But, rather like joy, thanksgiving 'in all circumstances' comes through focusing on the great unchanging realities of God in Christ, the unchangeable temporal and eternal blessings of the gospel and the constantly available privileges of being a Christian. Ours is not the joy and thanksgiving of a fake triumphalism, a false light-heartedness, but the 'solid joys and lasting treasures none but Zion's children know'.

Questions

1. Without a critical spirit, assess the strengths and weaknesses of the fellowship you belong to in the light of these verses. Is there anything amiss? Any weakness to be strengthened? Any strength to be fostered?
2. How can you be joyful if you don't feel joyful?
3. What do you find easy and what do you find difficult about keeping times of prayer and about making prayer a constant factor in life? Have you any tips to share? The Lord Jesus deliberately withdrew to pray (Luke 5:15–16; 6:12). He used the early morning (Mark 1:35) and the late evening (Mark 6:35, 46); he could 'pray alone' even in company (Luke 11:1).

1 Thessalonians 5:19–22

Available powers

The Holy Spirit, prophecies and discernment are all factors that are on our side as we live obedient lives in readiness for the Lord's return.

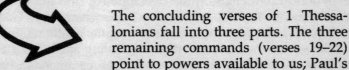 The concluding verses of 1 Thessalonians fall into three parts. The three remaining commands (verses 19–22) point to powers available to us; Paul's prayer (verses 23–24) points to the unceasing work of God to perfect us in holiness in readiness for the return of the Lord Jesus; and verses 25–28 are a veritable cluster of strengthening things – mutual prayer, loving fellowship, hearing God's word, indwelling grace.

As the 'Stop and look' section on page 102 shows, the commands which began at verse 12 consist of five groups of three. Here are the final three: they deal with the Holy Spirit, prophecies and spiritual discernment.

The Holy Spirit (verse 19)

Many assume that the command not to 'put out the Spirit's fire' implies that some within the Thessalonian church were exercising dramatic 'gifts of the Spirit' and that Paul was here weighing in on their side against others who were belittling such manifestations. This may be so, but it is, in fact, reading a lot into a very few words and is far from the most natural way of looking at them.

Matthew 3:11–12 refers to the Holy Spirit as fire. In that passage the Holy Spirit is the Lord's purifying agent, creating a purged people for him. Acts 2:1–4 describes the initial coming of the Holy Spirit in his fourfold action: how he came, first, into the world: he 'filled the whole house'; secondly, he rested 'on each of them', enduing individuals with the Holy Spirit; thirdly, they were 'filled with the Holy Spirit', specially empowered for a particular task; fourthly, they 'began to speak in other tongues' or languages, the particular gift of the Spirit, creating them into a missionary people able to communicate God's truth intelligibly.

As in Matthew, the Holy Spirit as fire comes to create a special people for the Lord. Matthew focuses on their purity, Acts on their ability. There has been a very strong emphasis on holiness in 1 Thessalonians (1:5–6; 3:13; 4:3–4, 7–8) and in particular on the development of a life of holy obedience. In 4:8 Paul followed up his insistence that God's will (4:3) is that we should be holy with the gentle reminder of the gift of the Holy Spirit. Here, having spelled out the will of God (4:18) in many practical commands, Paul reminds us that the Holy One is present to create a holy people for the Lord.

The word of God (verse 20)

Once more we must try to resist the temptation to create a large scenario around a very few words, and try rather to reach a central understanding of what Paul actually says.

In Acts 2 the immediate consequence of the coming of the Holy Spirit was 'prophecy'. In order to explain what was amazing those who were present, Peter appealed to Joel 2:28–32: the outpouring of the Lord's Spirit followed by men and women alike 'prophesying'. In Acts 2:11, what each heard, intelligibly, in varying languages, was 'the wonders of God'. Surely we are not mistaken in thinking that in his sermon Peter spelled out in detail what those wonders were: the Lord Jesus in his death, resurrection and ascension. Joel's prophecy ended with the words, 'Everyone who calls on the name of the Lord will be saved' (Acts 2:21); Peter ended his sermon with, 'God has made this Jesus, whom you crucified ... Lord.'

Peter's words can be taken as a perfect example of what, by grace, must have been happening all over that early church. They did not possess the whole written Scripture; they constantly needed inspired utterance to take (what we call) the Old Testament and to show how it was fulfilled in the Lord Jesus. Prophets did other things as well, of course (Acts 11:27–30; 21:10–11). But, as with their Old Testament counterparts, their main task was to declare the truth about God.

Paul has called us to practical obedience. If we are to obey, we must constantly attend with loving reverence to our Father's word – which, to us, is the now completed Bible – and we must be ready to give close, unwearied attention to those whom he calls to teach us the word of God. Negatively, Paul says, 'do not treat ... with contempt'. Of course, once Paul left Thessalonica they were dependent for 'prophecy' on their own members. Did Satan tempt them to say something about someone who stood up to minister? 'What would he know about it? Why, what is he but the milkman!' The Corinthians similarly treated Paul and his ministry as insignificant (2 Corinthians 10:10) –

using the same Greek word as here.

In our own case, we have the word of God read in our services, but how many people, over coffee immediately after the service, could say what passage had been read and what it was about? Many churches are blessed with a serious and attractive ministry of Holy Scripture and people are rapt in their attention to the preaching – but could they repeat on Monday what they heard on Sunday? Yet, with the Spirit of God who aids us to hold on to the revealed truth (2 Timothy 1:14), the word of God is our major resource in keeping his commandments.

Personal moral and spiritual discernment (verse 21)

The three commands here are really one: everything must be tested with a view to holding the good and refusing evil. This is the way the Bereans (Paul's next port of call after Thessalonica) responded. According to Acts, they were 'of more noble character', and they showed this nobility in the way they examined the Scriptures every day to see if what Paul said was true (Acts 17:11). They did exactly what Paul now commands us: to develop and exercise spiritual discernment; to accept nothing because someone says so, but always to go back to base in Scripture.

In Matthew 7:21, 23 the Lord Jesus warns us that even seemingly spiritual activities may actually be without spiritual substance – and be seen to be so when faced with the crucial question, 'Do they produce holiness? Do they change people morally and spiritually from evildoing?' John warns that not every spirit abroad in the world is the Holy Spirit. The spirits must be tested with questions about Jesus. Is he confessed as the truly incarnate God (1 John 4:1–2)? Is Jesus acknowledged as Lord, the truly divine one (1 Corinthians 12:3)?

All this is exercising the spiritual discernment which guards us from evil and leads us to hold 'on to the good'. This is our own personal spiritual responsibility for our own spiritual well-being.

Yet, though we must indeed take up our responsibility in

this way, we are very far from being on our own. Look back: we have the Holy Spirit on our side (verse 19) and we have the word of God to nourish and direct (verse 20).

Questions

1. In what ways would you say we possess the Holy Spirit's fire? Is it a fact or a feeling or both? How might we be in danger of putting the fire out?
2. Did prophecy stop when the New Testament was completed? Is there still prophecy today? For guidance see the feature on 'Prophets' below.
3. What tests should we apply to decide whether a statement is true or false, wise or foolish? Take a statement like 'Christians should not keep company with unbelievers'. How should we understand it?

Prophets

In Acts we meet a prophet in the person of Agabus, who was gifted by God with a predictive ability.

► In Acts 11:27–30 his prediction was followed through by the church, and when the famine came they were in a position to respond to the needs it created.

► In 21:10–11 his prediction turned out to be true, but Paul ignored it.

Thus we see that such predictions did not carry an unquestioned directive authority with them. In Acts 11:29 it says that following the prediction the disciples 'decided', that is to say, they discussed and came to a conclusion. The prediction was not a divine direction.

Prophecy in 1 Corinthians 14:29–33 would seem to be not prediction but the declaration of some truth from and of

God – as seems to be the case in 1 Thessalonians 5:20. Throughout 1 Corinthians 14, Paul's desire is that, in whatever way God shall choose, the gathered assembly should be edified by the intelligible truth (verses 4–5, 11, 17, 19). In this, the prophets have their part – as we suggested above – bringing the truth about Jesus to light in the context of the Scriptures they possessed. Of these prophets Paul says three things:

1 Their ministry must be orderly in presentation and restricted in quantity (verses 26, 29, 33).
2 They must not claim an uncontrollable impulse. Each prophet has control of his or her own spirit (verse 32): the uncontrolled and disorderly is not of God.
3 When such a prophet speaks, the others should exercise discernment, or 'weigh carefully what is said' (verse 29 – the same idea, though not the same word, as in 1 Thessalonians 5:21). The prophet's message does not possess automatic, directive, divine authority over the church. It is a human attempt to express divine truth. Note that when Paul commanded his letter to be read (1 Thessalonians 5:27), there was nothing about exercising discernment: the apostolic word is God's word (1 Corinthians 2:6–13).

The references to prophets in Ephesians 2:20; 3:5 may or may not belong to this same category. In each case we could easily understand Paul to be referring to 'the apostles and the prophets before them'. The Old Testament was the 'prophetic' period of revelation: thus Hebrews 1:1 and 2 Peter 1:20 can look back over the whole Old Testament period as prophetic/prophecy, the declaration of the truth about God through his chosen and inspired agents. In parallel, the New Testament is the 'apostolic' period, with the task of bringing the inspired word given to apostles and apostolic men. Alternatively, Paul may be referring to apostles as the foundational agents in revelation and the prophets as those gifted by God within local churches to bring out and apply scriptural truth in the light of Christ.

But there were and are false prophets. Indeed, John says that 'many false prophets have gone out into the world' (1 John 4:1), and Peter agrees (2 Peter 2:1).

False prophets can be known by their teaching: Peter notes their denial of the saving work of Christ (2 Peter 2:1); John, their denial of the reality of Christ's birth and life as Man and God (1 John 4:2). This corresponds with Deuteronomy 13:5, where the false prophet is exposed preaching 'rebellion against the LORD your God, who brought you out of Egypt and redeemed you' (compare Jeremiah 23:9–29).

There is also the practical test of Deuteronomy 18:21–22: the prediction which is not fulfilled is 'a message the LORD has not spoken'. Under the old covenant the false prophet was put to death (Deuteronomy 13:5). This indicated (not supposed Old Testament severity but) the seriousness of the sin involved – the misrepresentation of the Lord and the deception of his people. The words of the Lord Jesus are as important today as when he spoke them: that we should take care *how* and *what* we hear (Mark 4:24; Luke 8:18). When many believe themselves to have been given the gift of prophecy and so much of their ministry is predictive, it is a matter of importance that they should be heard with the discernment Paul enjoined, and that if their prediction is not fulfilled, the public nature of the prediction should be matched by public retraction and repentance and the imposition of discipline.

1 Thessalonians 5:23–24

Paul's prayer

Paul's prayer begins and ends with what God is.

God is 'the God of peace' (verse 23; see Romans 15:33; 16:20; Philippians 4:9; Hebrews 13:20). He is also the 'faithful' God (verse 24; see 1 Corinthians 1:9; 10:13; 2 Corinthians 1:18; 2 Thessalonians 3:3; 2 Timothy 2:13).

'Peace' was one of the earliest words Paul wrote to the Thessalonians (1:1), and we saw there that 'peace' is comprehensive completeness. It is peace with God, peace in the fellowship, and the peace of personal fulfilment. Ultimately – in heaven – it is the full reality of peace with God, free of the distractions, temptations and clouded fellowship with him that we experience on earth; a love of brothers and sisters without any whiff of disharmony or the slightest dislocation of oneness; a perfectly whole and integrated personality without those conflicting forces within, warring in our members (James 4:1) and setting mind and sinful nature at odds (Romans 7:25). Since all this is broadly what Paul is going to pray that God will do for us (verse 23), he starts by reminding us that, as the God of peace, God already has in his own nature all that is required to make us perfect.

Furthermore, because he is faithful he will not leave us until he has done what he promised (Genesis 28:15).

Between these opening and closing statements about what God *is* comes what he can and will *do* (verse 23). As in 3:13, the Father has the coming of the Son as his great objective. In human terms, if any one of our children is coming home we want everything just right: the room prepared as she would wish it; the menu planned to include what we know he likes. It is precious to parents to have everything perfect for their children. Will it not be so for Jesus when he comes? Will the Father leave anything undone, anything unready, anything less than perfect, anything that would fail to bring delight to him who is 'my son, whom I love' (Mark 1:11; 9:7)?

Consequently the Father, 'God himself', is taking us in hand. He will *sanctify*, 'make us holy', that is to say, make us like himself, the holy God. The image of God in which we were first created (Genesis 1:26–28), and which was marred and scarred by sin, will be restored (Ephesians 4:24). This 'making holy' deals totally (verse 23, 'through and through ... whole') with our total persons, 'spirit, soul and body'. If we are meant to probe some distinction in these words, then

▶ *spirit* is the self Godward

▶ *soul* is our inward nature, the unseen reality which is one aspect of our self

▶ and *bodies* are the outward and visible self.

All that we are was redeemed by Jesus and all will be presented to him in perfect holiness.

And there will be no 'slip 'twixt cup and lip'. He is the keeping God (verse 23). 'Kept' is a singular verb, because spirit, soul and body are the indivisible unity of the total person. *Blameless* means irreproachable in the light of some given standard – as Paul (Philippians 3:6) or Zechariah and Elizabeth (Luke 1:6) were irreproachable when judged by the standard of the law. But on the day of Christ the standard will be likeness to Christ – and we will be 'blameless'. What a work of God to achieve this! What a God to bend himself to the task! What a Jesus to resemble!

Questions

1. Is 'peace' just an inner feeling, such as can be achieved by

such things as meditation or enjoying a sunset? What is the peace of which Paul speaks?

2. Is it enough to say that peace is when a church is working smoothly without objections or argumentative groups? What would you add?

3. Or is peace when nations are not at war? Or when people have enough money for basic living? What does the 'God of peace' mean to us? Try to define what peace means personally, in the church and in the world.

1 Thessalonians 5:25–28

Goodbye!

A cameo of the model church.

Paul considered the church at Thessalonica as a model church in its evangelistic zeal (1:7). But now, in the light of all he has written, the picture of the ideal becomes a lovely fourfold reality:

▶ a church active in prayer ('Brothers, pray')

▶ a church full ('all') of mutual love ('holy kiss')

▶ a church gathered round the word of God ('have this letter read')

▶ a church founded in and fed by grace ('the grace of our Lord Jesus Christ').

The praying church. Paul was busy in prayer for them (1:2), and now he closes the brackets by asking them to pray for him (verse 25). Mutual prayer is love-at-a-distance, one of the bonds holding the people of God together. It is as much the duty of the led (verse 25) as of the leader (1:2).

The loving church. Christians should and may greet each other with a holy kiss – the kiss of love (1 Peter 5:14), free of sexual desire, that is the mark of family membership, the symbol of the unity of the community under one heavenly Father (Romans 16:16; 1 Corinthians 16:20; 2 Corinthians 13:12).

The listening church. Notice how forceful verse 27 is: 'I charge you' is 'I put you on oath.' Paul gave his letter the status of holy Scripture (Colossians 4:16). Just as our last glimpse of the church of the old covenant is of people gathered round the word of God (Nehemiah 8), so also we see the Thessalonian church and, through them, we see what a New Testament church essentially is: a congregation of believers around the word of God.

The nourished church (verse 28). Again a first word becomes the last word. In verse 23, 'peace' closed a bracket with 1:1. Now 'grace' fulfils the same function. As we saw at 1:1, 'grace' is not a 'something' which God injects into us – a sort of spiritual hypodermic. Grace is 'God being gracious'; it is God himself drawing near and sharing himself with us, in love, in salvation, in life-giving, in protecting, in providing. At the beginning it was the church 'in God the Father and the Lord Jesus Christ' (1:1). At the end it is the perfecting work of the Father (verses 23–24) and the sufficient grace of the Lord Jesus Christ (verse 28).

Questions

1. Paul puts listening seriously to the word of God ('do not treat prophecies with contempt') side by side with holding the good and avoiding the evil. This suggests that every 'hearing of the word' – private reading, listening to the Scriptures being read, the preaching of the word – should be followed by thoughtful application. How can we best do this individually and as a church?

2. Is the grace of our Lord Jesus Christ totally absent from the world outside the church? How do we receive his grace for daily personal and communal life?
3. Suppose that your group (or you personally) had the task of presenting the message of 1 Thessalonians to the rest of your church during a worship session or service. How would you do it, with imagination, clarity and relevance for today? Think creatively. Then try to find an opportunity to put your ideas into practice.

Stop and look: what is 2 Thessalonians all about?

Time has moved on a little. If 1 Thessalonians was written fairly soon after Paul's time in the city, this second letter comes after a further gap of perhaps just a few months, maybe less than that. Paul has heard further news of the Christians in Thessalonica; maybe he had sent Timothy there again (1 Thessalonians 3:1–2). Some of the news is good (1:3), but not all of it. Paul is concerned that they may be taking up wrong ideas about the second coming of Jesus (2:2), in spite of all the teaching he gave them on it, both when he was with them and in his first letter (2:15). Also, he is worried that some of them have not listened to his encouragement about work in 1 Thessalonians 4:11–12.

So he dashes off this little letter to them – only 822 words long, but packed full of nourishment. As usual with Paul, every single word counts. It looks as though he had kept a copy of his first letter, and reminded himself of what he had written before writing again, because there are lots of reminders of 1 Thessalonians here. His letter has four parts to it:

1:1–12   He greets them, praises them and gives them a powerful summary of *the shape of the Christian life*, emphasizing the future coming of the Lord Jesus.

2:1–12   He tackles the worrying news he has heard and repeats the teaching he gave, while with them, about *the 'rebellion' and the coming of Jesus*.

2:13 – 3:5   He encourages them in the light of the rather frightening picture he has painted, prays for them and teaches them about *belonging to Jesus in the meantime*.

3:6–18   He turns to the problem of sponging. Some
          church members have been misusing fellow-
          ship and depending on their wealthier brothers
          to support them. Paul tells them that, waiting
          for Jesus to return, it's *business as usual*!

But the great burden of this letter, its dominant theme, is
the second coming of Jesus Christ. Above all else, Paul wants
the Thessalonians to get their thinking straight about this,
and to order their lives around expecting it. But what about
us? We are writing this study guide approximately 1,950
years after Paul wrote this letter. And still Jesus has not
come. Should we still be waiting, with urgent expectation?
Generally speaking, like the queue at the bus stop near our
home, we have lost heart and drifted away. Expectation has
faded, and the church of Jesus Christ is no longer waiting
longingly for his return. Isn't that true?

Ask yourself when you last heard a Christian leader
speak passionately about Jesus' second coming. And if you
heard one recently, ask yourself: How did I respond? Did
you get passionate about it too, or, like many others, did
you feel a little uneasy, not wanting to be a crank? On your
mental list of 'ten things I'd hate my boss to know about
me', how far up the list does 'I believe that Jesus Christ will
come to earth again, appearing to the whole world simul-
taneously' come? Is it above or below 'I think the boss's wife
is one of the ugliest women I've met'?

And be honest: how much does the second coming of
Jesus actually impact upon our daily lives as Christians, and
on our church activities and teaching programmes? Even if
'officially' we still believe it, it has faded from prominence.

Recently, a particular evangelistic programme has become popular in Britain and has spread to other countries
too. It features about fifteen sessions giving a basic introduction to the Christian faith. In many ways it is excellent
and many have become Christians through it. But in it the
second coming of Jesus is not taught or explained at all. The
reason is not that the compilers of the course have stopped
believing in it. It is just that it isn't relevant (apparently) to

the heart of Christian faith and life today. It's non-essential.

But Paul would disagree *passionately* with this. His initial teaching programme to the newborn Thessalonian church *majored* on the second coming, and so do both his letters to them. Have things changed so much, that what was essential then is non-essential now? I think (as we will see) that Paul might indeed be surprised that we have waited so long. But he would have an explanation for the delay; it's here in 2 Thessalonians for us to discover. And I believe that he would lay as much emphasis today as then on *right thinking* about the second coming, and on *right lifestyle* in view of the End which is still to be.

Yes, it's amazing how much he packs into 822 words.

THE SHAPE OF THE
CHRISTIAN LIFE

2 Thessalonians 1:1–12

2 Thessalonians 1:1–4

Hello and thanks

Paul greets his Thessalonians with love and genuine thankfulness for their growth in faith and love.

The opening greeting (1:1–2) is exactly the same as in 1 Thessalonians, except for the addition of the last phrase, 'from God the Father and the Lord Jesus Christ'. As phrased in 1 Thessalonians 1:1–2, the greeting might just convey the impression that somehow Paul, Silas and Timothy could give 'grace and peace' to the Thessalonians. Now there can be no mistake: this 'grace and peace' can come only from their Father God and the Lord Jesus together.

Why? Because grace and peace are to do with our relationship with them. And we cannot get ourselves into grace and peace with God. Our 'natural' relationship with God is offence and distance. With many others, I love C. S. Lewis's *Narnia* stories – and one of my favourites is the story of the 'Dufflepuds' in *The Voyage of the Dawn Treader*. The Dufflepuds hop around on one large foot which doubles as an umbrella when they fall asleep. Lucy and the others quickly discover that they are harmless, but living in fear of the mad invisible Wizard who rules their island and is always trying to trick them. But the true picture emerges when Lucy meets the Wizard, and discovers that he is gentle and kind, and has been appointed by Aslan to educate the Dufflepuds out of their hostility and fear. They agree that he has an enormous job on his hands. The more the Wizard tries to offer them friendship, the more the Dufflepuds suspect a trap.

Like the Wizard and the Dufflepuds, God offers us 'grace' and 'peace' with himself. On God's behalf, Paul, Silas and Timothy offer it to the Thessalonians in this greeting (see 2 Corinthians 5:20). And then Paul repeats his prayer at the end of the letter (2 Thessalonians 3:16, 18) – so that, like his first letter, this one both begins and ends with 'grace' and 'peace' (see 1 Thessalonians 5:23, 28). Will the Thessalonians receive the gift?

Paul thanks God that, at the moment at any rate, they are certainly receiving it (verses 3–4). He thanks God for their growing 'faith' and 'love'. These are the human qualities which mark our response to 'grace' and 'peace' from God. C. S. Lewis doesn't extend the story, but we can imagine the fantastic breakthrough when, for the thousandth time, the Wizard says, 'Look – I'm really not an ogre, and I really don't want to harm you. Can you accept that?' and into the silence which follows a small Dufflepud voice says, 'OK. I'll buy that.' Grace must be matched by faith, trust.

As soon as that happens, peace breaks out – a whole new relationship in which the Dufflepuds can begin to love the Wizard as their Father. Paul thanks God that the Thessalonians' faith is 'growing more and more', and their love 'increasing'. He is probably thinking back to his earlier letter, which he began in a similar way (1 Thessalonians 1:3; compare 3:6), and in which he urged them to love each other 'more and more' (4:10). Now he thanks God that they've done it.

Paul's love for them is very clear. Like every true pastor the world over, he is deeply delighted by their growth in faith and love. As we will see, he was also deeply concerned about them, but an awareness of the negative does not rub out the positive. 'We [ourselves] boast about you,' he says emphatically (verse 4) – probably looking back to 1 Thessalonians 1:8, where he said that he didn't need to report their faith to the other churches, because their reputation had gone before them. Now, he says, I can't help joining in the chorus of praise!

How is faith expressed? We could list several obvious ways – prayer, worship, reciting a creed, witnessing to nonbelievers, getting baptized. But Paul has none of these in mind when he thinks about the growth in the Thessalonians' faith. It's their 'perseverance' and their faithfulness through 'all the persecutions and trials you are enduring' (verse 4) – this is what *really* shows their faith. They faced persecution as soon as they became Christians (Acts 17:1–9; 1 Thessalonians 1:6; 2:14), and it didn't stop. Concerned for their survival, Paul sent Timothy to encourage them and to 'find out about [their] faith' (1 Thessalonians 3:2–5). Now we discover that the persecution is still going on, probably months later. But their faith has grown stronger, and Paul rejoices.

Many churches face threatening opposition in the world today – the sort of opposition which can so easily turn into physical harm, arrest of leaders, loss of employment, burning of buildings, even murder. Paul's heart bled for the Thessalonians, but his chief concern was not the pain but the possibility that the devil might use the persecution to ruin their faith, 'and all our labour might come to nothing' (1 Thessalonians 3:5). For he faced dreadful persecution too (1 Thessalonians 3:7), and he knew that Christians can come through any kind of trial with their faith strengthened, their love deepened, even their joy increased. That's still true.

Questions

1. Try to compose a modern parable to illustrate the meaning of 'grace' and 'peace' from God through Jesus.
2. Paul 'accentuates the positive' in his praise of the Thessalonians. How may we do this effectively in our relationships with each other – while (if necessary) also being aware of the negative in others?
3. Concerned at the persecution they were facing, Paul sent

Timothy to strengthen the Thessalonians. In what practical, realistic ways can we show our fellowship and support for Christians facing persecution in other places?

2 Thessalonians 1:5–10

When will the mess get sorted?

We live in a messy world: a world in which the children of the Creator get persecuted for their loyalty to him. Will it ever be sorted out? How?

Paul was an enthusiast. His thoughts tumble over each other, clamouring for expression – and so his thanksgiving just bubbles on through one long opening sentence (157 words!), in which he reveals his heart. In these verses we hear the things which, above all else, he wanted the Thessalonians to grasp.

Though they just come pouring out, these verses have a careful pattern:

A Future salvation for the Thessalonians (1:5)
  B Future judgment for their persecutors (1:6)
    C The future coming of the Lord Jesus (1:7)
  B^1 Future punishment for the disobedient (1:8–9)
A^2 Future salvation for believers (1:10)

Verse 7 expresses the central thought: the 'revelation' of the Lord Jesus is the key future event on the horizon of world history. Paul emphasizes it with the very last phrase of this long sentence in verse 10: 'on the Day' (moved to the beginning of verse 10 in NIV).

'That day' is the peg on which hangs the destiny of all people. Will they be 'worthy of the kingdom of God' (verse 5) which Jesus will then establish? Or will they receive 'everlasting destruction' and exclusion from his presence (verse 9)? This doesn't depend on an arbitrary decision by God. Not only Jesus in person but the *truth* will be revealed on that Day – the truth about the relationship of each person to the God who then steps into the history of his world to bring it to completion. At the moment, it's all loose ends, change, potential, growth and setback, lack of justice, suffering for the good and prosperity for the wicked. But then ... people's choices for or against their relationship with God will finally be fixed, and the consequences experienced.

Paul's teaching here can seem very black and white. It doesn't fit a postmodern age in which everything's OK, so long as it feels good. Why should Jesus 'punish' (verse 8, literally 'give vengeance') in this harsh way? Doesn't he tell us to forgive? Why can't he do so, then?

The answer takes us to the heart of this passage. We can summarize Paul's teaching like this:

God will rescue his suffering church. Your present faith and perseverance, says Paul, are 'evidence' (or 'a sign') of God's righteous judgment. Why? Because God will certainly save his people. We sometimes wonder how suffering can fit with God's loving, and sovereign, will for us. But here sufferings are a *proof* that one day God will intervene. 'Will not God bring about justice for his chosen ones, who cry to him day and night? Will he keep putting them off?' said Jesus (Luke 18:7; see also Philippians 1:27–28, Revelation 6:9–11).

God's 'righteous judgment' confirms the choices people have made. He allows us to choose our relationship with him, and respects our choice. He does not – cannot – impose warm feelings towards himself upon creatures who refuse to know him. To those who 'trouble' (persecute) his church, he will give 'trouble' (verse 6, compare Romans 2:5–9). To those who finally refuse to know him through the gospel of the Lord Jesus, he will give the exclusion from his presence which they have chosen (verses 8–9). It's awfully, finally, horribly simple – and ultimately depends on our dignity as responsible human beings. If we respond to his grace, we can be creatures of heaven. If we reject his love, we will be food for hell.

Both rescue and judgment will be given by Jesus when he 'appears'. Jesus steps into God's role here – as Paul makes clear by drawing language from Isaiah 66:15–16 in verse 8. He is also drawing on Jesus' own teaching in Mark 13:26–27 as he expresses his conviction that Jesus will return, to be God's agent in finally redeeming his world: finally ridding it of sin, finally establishing his kingdom. Ultimately God's moral order will prevail. The bombers and wreckers will be brought to justice. There is meaning, and right, in the universe, after all! But at the moment the bombers and wreckers get away with it. No human system of justice is sufficient. We need Jesus to bring the judgment of God, to rescue the innocent and condemn the wicked (unless they repent first).

There will be glory for the Lord Jesus and his church together. In verse 10 Paul again applies an Old Testament picture of God to Jesus. In Psalm 89:7, the Septuagint, the Greek Old Testament, pictures God 'being glorified in the council of his holy ones'. There the 'holy ones' are, of course, the angels. But when Paul applies this picture to Jesus, the 'holy ones' now include the church, caught up into his presence (remember 1 Thessalonians 4:17) and becoming part of his glorious retinue.

The last part of verse 10 would be better translated, 'And all because you believed our testimony to you!' In obedience to Jesus' instruction in Mark 13:9, Paul had borne 'testimony' in hostile Thessalonica, the church was born, and simply because of their faith in that testimony the Thessalonians will join the procession – on that Day!

Questions

1. Supposing Jesus came tomorrow ... think realistically

and carefully about the effect of his coming on your town and neighbourhood. What would happen? Can you imagine it?

2. What connection does this passage suggest between the coming of Jesus and the preaching of the gospel?

3. Imagine you've got Paul attending your group meeting. Ask him: 'Paul, why do you lay such emphasis on the second coming of Jesus?' What is his reply?

Eternal destruction?

This is what Paul predicts in 2 Thessalonians 1:8–9 for all who 'do not know God, and do not obey the gospel of our Lord Jesus'. What exactly does he mean by it? In recent years two viewpoints have been supported:

▶ Either Paul means that, finally, the unsaved will cease to exist completely, or

▶ Paul means that the unsaved will continue to exist, but in a state of never-ending punishment and exclusion from the presence of God which can be called 'destruction'.

Supporters of the second viewpoint feel that the first one undermines evangelism and downplays the clear teaching of Scripture. After all, why should we strive to save the lost if in the end they don't get punished but simply cease to exist? And isn't ultimate punishment clearly taught by Jesus (*e.g.* Matthew 25:46)?

Supporters of the first viewpoint feel that the second one does not think clearly enough about the nature of 'life'. After all, God is the source of all life. He gives it (Romans 4:17) and sustains it through Jesus (Hebrews 1:3). So final exclusion from his presence must mean the final extinction of life.

Paul uses this word 'destruction' also in 1 Thessalonians

5:3. We saw in our study on that passage the comment of one writer that there it means 'not destruction of being but of well-being, not putting an end to the existence of a person but its ruin so far as the purpose of its existence is concerned'. The word is used several times in the Septuagint (the Greek Old Testament), usually in contexts which speak of the judgment of God, and usually implying physical death (*e.g.* 1 Kings 13:34; Jeremiah 51:54–55; Ezekiel 14:16). But sometimes it is used as an equivalent of 'ruin', or 'disaster', without necessarily implying physical death (*e.g.* Proverbs 1:26; Obadiah 13).

When Paul adds the word 'eternal' to it, how does that affect its meaning? The basic meaning of 'eternal' is not so much 'everlasting' as 'of the age to come'. So we could paraphrase 'eternal destruction' as 'the kind of ruin, disaster and destruction that come upon people in the age to come'. But what kind of ruin is that? Is it total extinction, or everlasting punishment? The phrase itself does not help us to answer this question.

There are several other passages of Scripture that relate to this, and to do justice to the question we ought to study them all: Matthew 8:12; 25:46; Mark 9:47–48; Luke 16:22–24; Romans 2:7–9; 9:22; Revelation 20:6–15. But even if we did so, we might feel in the long run that it was impossible to decide, on the basis of these scriptures, whether the unsaved continue in never-ending conscious torment or not.

But do we really need to know? The important point is that 'destruction' is a ghastly prospect for any human being, whatever it actually consists of. Finally to be excluded from the only source of life, joy and fulfilment – how terrible! The thought that God had provided a way of salvation from this destiny sent Paul scurrying round the Mediterranean in a passionate desire to spread the Good News as far as he could. And we still have the only message that can secure for human beings the life for which they were designed – life in intimate fellowship with their Creator. Anything less than this is ruin, disaster and destruction.

Paul's example challenges us to focus on the priority of proclaiming the gospel to lost people. If we let ourselves be sidetracked into passionate debates about the *fate* of the lost, we've missed the point.

2 Thessalonians 1:11–12

Class 1 priorities

Paul summarizes his constant prayer for the Thessalonians, and gives us a window into his absolute priorities for the Christian life.

Paul often describes his prayer for his readers, after the opening thanksgiving in his letters (see Romans 1:9; Ephesians 1:15ff.; Philippians 1:4; Colossians 1:9–
12; 2 Timothy 1:3; Philemon 6). And in all these places, as here, he says that his prayer is 'constant' or 'unceasing' (see also 1 Thessalonians 1:2–3). He opens his pastor's heart and reveals the love that kept him constantly talking to God about his churches.

He illustrates what he means as he writes this letter. On three occasions, during the writing of it, he bursts into prayer for the Thessalonians: 2:16–17; 3:5 and 3:16. These prayers make a fascinating study in themselves.

But what we have here is not a prayer but a prayer-report – that is, a summary of all his prayers for them. If you collected all his many moments of prayer, and combined them into one, short prayer summarizing all of them, what would it be? That's the kind of prayer we have here. So in this prayer we can see Paul's essential priorities for the Thessalonians, the goals which above all he wants them to attain in their Christian lives. What are they?

He prays for three things – notice 'that … that … so that'

in the NIV. These three prayers relate to their characters, their activities, and their relationship with each other and with Jesus.

Characters matching God's 'call' (verse 11a)

Paul prays that God will 'make [not "count", NIV] you worthy of his calling'. God's 'calling' is his intention that the Thessalonians should participate in that victory parade when Jesus comes again. He 'calls' them – and us – to that destiny. But Paul knows that the Thessalonians cannot make themselves worthy to join that procession. So he prays that God will do it, 'by his power'. (This phrase in the second half of the verse actually covers both the prayers in verse 11, not just the second one.)

We remember his prayer in 1 Thessalonians 5:23: 'May God … sanctify you through and through. May your whole spirit, soul and body be kept blameless at the coming of our Lord Jesus Christ.' We remember too Jesus' parable of the wedding feast, and the man who failed to wear the right clothes (Matthew 22:1–13). Although the invitation was so open and free, so that there were no entrance qualifications for the feast, yet the guests still had to be dressed in a way that honoured their host and his generosity.

So for us. We need to be 'dressed' in the fruit of the Spirit (Galatians 5:22), our characters made 'worthy' to be on display when Jesus comes again – as evidence of the effectiveness of his work as Saviour. We must work at putting on these clothes – but we'll need God's power if we want to succeed.

Actions arising from love of goodness, and from faith (verse 11b)

Paul's second prayer is again for God's power to be at work in them – this time enabling them really to turn desire into action, every time their heart moves them to express 'goodness' or 'faith' in practical action.

Paul actually uses the word 'goodness' here, which, with

'faith', appears in the list of the fruit of the Spirit in
Galatians 5:22. So many good intentions come to nothing, in
the church of Jesus Christ. One of the devil's sharpest
strategies, as he tries to frustrate God's work, is to intervene
between intention and performance. If, by any means, he
can stop us from *actually* getting up to pray, mounting a
children's holiday club, starting a care programme for the
elderly, running a mission, getting to know our neighbours
... then the 'goodness' and 'faith' which prompted the
desire are frustrated, and the fruit might wither on the
branch. That's what he hopes.

So Paul prays that God will give them success at this
crucial point of turning desire into action.

Paul does not actually mention the Holy Spirit in verse
11. But the work of the Spirit is implicit here: for it is he who
creates holiness (compare 1 Thessalonians 4:7–8), and he
who enables the practice of his fruit (compare 1 Thessalonians 1:4–6).

Glory for the Lord Jesus (verse 12)

Paul's third prayer picks up God's supreme motivation, in
everything he does for us and in us: it is all for the glory of
Jesus.

What is this glory? It probably has two aspects to it:

▶ It is *the glory he will receive when he returns*, when he
will be 'marvelled at' by believers (verse 10) and
exalted as Judge and Saviour. It is the public
acclamation of this now visible Lord, bringing the
kingdom of God and receiving the worship of the
world.

▶ It is *the glory he receives now*, when the church
worships him as 'Lord', and others catch the bug and
start to worship too, seeing the effect he has on the
lives of believers.

'And you in him,' Paul adds. God's grace is such that, as
we saw in verse 10, the glory of the Lord Jesus is spread and

shared among his followers, like the crowds of cheering football supporters who fill the streets, basking in the reflected glory of their team's success as they return home.

Questions

1. What can we really do to change our characters? Some people say we are stuck with being the way we are. Is that true?
2. Someone said: 'When Christians are thinking about outreach, they should stop asking for guidance ("What *should* we do?"), and start asking for power ("What *can* we do?").' Do you think this is good advice?
3. Think globally: what must Christians do above all else, do you think, in order to bring glory to the name ('Lord') of Jesus in the next ten years? – assuming that he does not return!

THE 'REBELLION'
AND THE COMING
OF JESUS

2 Thessalonians 2:1–12

Stop and look: what is happening in 2:1–12?

This is the next section of the letter. Paul turns from his glowing opening greeting and prayer to the first of the two things that concern him about the Thessalonians. We could well have gathered the hint from 1:6–10 that it's about the second coming of Jesus.

Paul is concerned that they may have heard a false idea about the second coming, and that it may even have been attached to his own name as authority (verse 2). How could this have come about, in a church to which he had so recently given so much teaching on this subject?

The answer may lie in the possible existence of a letter falsely claiming Paul as its author. This happened frequently in the ancient world, though usually after the death of a great figure. All sorts of works, supposedly by Paul and other apostles, were written and circulated during the second century. But Paul is clearly worried that this may have started already, during his lifetime. Verse 2 reads most naturally as a warning against something they *may* hear, rather than an attack on something he knows they *have* heard.

The false idea is that the Day of the Lord has already come. Paul proves to the Thessalonians that this cannot be right, by pointing to a massive event which must happen first, before Jesus comes. He describes this event in detail in verses 3–10. But because he had already told the Thessalonians about it (verses 5–6), he does not explain the details, and this leaves us with quite a few puzzles. 2 Thessalonians 2:1–12 is in fact one of the most challenging chapters in all Paul's letters, so you may need to invest a little more time in studying this section, especially if you are leading a group.

I take the view that, in a study guide like this, the best approach is not to discuss all the various interpretations offered by different scholars and writers, but simply to present the explanation of the passage that I have come to after much study and prayer. So please bear in mind, as you read, that others interpret the passage differently, and their books are available.

There is one vital point to make before we start to look at the passage in detail. This point comes to light when we ask: if the Thessalonians thought that the Day of the Lord had already come, then why didn't Paul just remind them of what he had written in 1 Thessalonians 4:13 – 5:11? There he described a very visible 'day of the Lord', complete with resurrection of the dead, archangel's voice, a meeting in the clouds and trumpets off. We could hear him asking, 'So – has that happened, then? It may have happened in Thessalonica, but we didn't notice it here in Corinth!'

Something obviously prompted him to re-emphasize this other aspect of his teaching, to which he doesn't refer in 1 Thessalonians. Why does he do it? We need to remember that, in his teaching in 1 Thessalonians 4:13 – 5:11, Paul was drawing upon the teaching of Jesus himself. He was reminding them of 'the Lord's own word' (1 Thessalonians 4:15: see above, p. 84). And all through that section we noticed many reminders of the teaching of Jesus recorded in Mark 13, Matthew 24 and Luke 21 (pp. 87–88, 93, 95). The same is true of 2 Thessalonians 2:1–12.

So the best answer to the question, 'Why does he say all this?' is simply, 'First, because this is what Jesus taught, and secondly, because it answers this wretched nonsense about the day of the Lord being past.' When tackling the problem of those who have died before Jesus' coming (1 Thessalonians 4:13), Paul focuses on the resurrection of the dead at Christ's return. But now he is tackling a different problem, and so he draws on different aspects of the teaching in Mark 13, Matthew 24 and Luke 21.

So, in order to interpret this section of 2 Thessalonians, we need to have Jesus' teaching clearly in mind. As we will see, Paul often alludes to it, as in 1 Thessalonians 4:13 – 5:11. So before studying this passage it's important to read through either Mark 13 or Matthew 24. You'll be struck by the differences as much as by the similarities, because Paul does not just repeat Jesus' teaching, but thinks it through afresh in the light of other scriptures. We'll trace all this as we go through it ourselves.

If you have the Crossway Bible Guide on Mark (by David Hewitt) or on Matthew (by Stephen Dray), it would be helpful to read the sections on Mark 13 (pp. 171–180) or on Matthew 24 (pp. 212–218).

2 Thessalonians 2:1–3a

Jesus *is* coming again

We too need to listen to Paul's firm teaching that the coming of Jesus is a future event, not a past experience.

It's certainly more difficult to believe in the second coming of Jesus now, almost two thousand years later, than it was for the first Christians. But even in the first Christian generation some began to question this expectation. Why did they do so?

Paul was writing 2 Thessalonians from Corinth. Some two years later, after he had finished his period of ministry there and moved on to Ephesus, he wrote back to the church in Corinth and criticized them for holding a view similar to the view he attacks here. He is worried that the Thessalonians may have started to believe 'that the Day of the Lord has already come' (verse 2). He asks the Corinthians, deeply concerned, 'How can some of you say that there is no resurrection of the dead?' (1 Corinthians 15:12).

We must remember that the resurrection of the dead and the second coming of Christ were closely connected for Paul

(1 Thessalonians 4:16). The Corinthians had not stopped believing in life after death – that is not the issue. They had stopped believing in a future event labelled 'the resurrection of the dead', because they believed it had already happened. So vivid was their experience of the risen Christ in worship, so vital their sense of the living power of the Holy Spirit, so impressive their use of supernatural spiritual gifts, that they felt as though they were in heaven already, raised from the dead. They thought the body didn't matter, and that at death they would just move a little closer to God, leaving this world of matter finally behind.

This may well be the teaching that Paul fears has spread from Corinth to Thessalonica, carried there perhaps even with his own authority claimed for it. He objects to it, not because it overemphasizes the experience of the Spirit, but because it underemphasizes the significance of this world. God is concerned with the world, not just with the church, as Paul shows in 2 Thessalonians 1:5–10. There must be final judgment on the wicked. And there must be (as Paul insists in 1 Corinthians 15) resurrection of the body as well as of the soul.

This denial of future resurrection has a surprisingly modern ring. In recent years even eminent church leaders have made it clear that they do not believe in the bodily resurrection of the Lord Jesus, because the vital thing is our *spiritual* encounter with him. The same people are quick to add that we need not believe in a literal second coming of Jesus, because (again) the vital thing is his coming to us now through the Spirit and in the church.

Do not be deceived

But according to Paul this is gravely mistaken. 'Don't let anyone deceive you,' he warns (verse 3a), echoing the same warning of Jesus himself in Mark 13:5 (Matthew 24:4; Luke 21:8): 'Watch out that no-one deceives you. Many will come in my name, saying, "I am he."' In this Corinthian idea about a *past* resurrection and day of the Lord, Paul hears the voice of a false Messiah which may deceive the Lord's people (see also Mark 13:22; Matthew 24:24).

Similarly in verse 2, Paul urges them 'not to become unsettled or alarmed' by such ideas. Here he uses a most unusual word, which also appears in Mark 13:7 (Matthew 24:6), as Jesus warns his disciples not to be 'alarmed' by reports of wars: 'Such things must happen,' he says, 'but the end is still to come.' So Paul uses this word as Jesus had done – to warn against a *false* excitement about the coming of the Lord, prompted either by dreadful world events (Mark 13) or false ideas about a non-literal 'coming' (2 Thessalonians 2).

Rather, Paul asks us to believe not only in a real 'coming' of the Lord Jesus as a future event, but also in 'our being gathered to him' (verse 1). Here again he uses an unusual word which likewise appears in Mark 13:27 and Matthew 24:31, of the angels gathering 'the elect' from the four corners of the earth at the coming of 'the Son of Man'. As he describes it in 1 Thessalonians 4:17, Paul clearly expected all believers to be gathered supernaturally to meet with Christ at his return – 'to meet the Lord in the air', as he puts it there. And because he uses 'we' and 'our' both there and here in 2 Thessalonians 2:1, we conclude that he expected this to happen, in all likelihood, during his own lifetime.

Paul actually has two concerns joined together here. Yes, the false teaching about the coming of Jesus is uppermost in his mind, but closely connected with this is his concern for their *stability* as Christians. 'Easily unsettled' (verse 2) is literally 'quickly shaken in mind'. Their stability is under threat enough, from the persecution they face. But here's a much more subtle threat, attacking them from within – a threat to their 'mind'. Paul knows that if their Christian thinking becomes disturbed, then their whole lives will be upset.

The joining of these two concerns here gives us the structure of the chapter: in verses 3b–12 he tackles the second-coming issue, then returns to the issue of their stability in verses 13–17.

Questions

1. Is belief in a literal second coming of Jesus really as essential as all that? Why?
2. Try to write a poem, compose a song or draw a picture – or just have a discussion – to express what it may be like at the moment of Jesus' return.
3. Do you think it's true that our *minds* are essential for our stability as Christians? In what ways? Why? What about those who are mentally disabled in some way? How can we make sure that we are thinking straight about our faith?

2 Thessalonians 2:3b–12

But first ... the coming of 'the lawless one'

Paul outlines the sequence of events which must take place first, before Jesus comes.

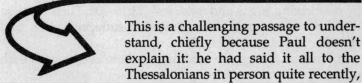

This is a challenging passage to understand, chiefly because Paul doesn't explain it: he had said it all to the Thessalonians in person quite recently, and now is just reminding them (verses 5–6). But once again Scripture itself comes to our rescue. We have already seen how Paul bases his own teaching about the End upon the teaching of Jesus himself. So now too, with Mark 13 and Matthew 24 as a kind of key, this difficult passage becomes clearer.

Paul tells the Thessalonians that, before 'the day of the Lord' can occur, something called 'the rebellion' must

145

happen. Along with, or after, the rebellion, 'the man of law-lessness' must appear (verse 3). This person will establish himself in 'God's temple, proclaiming himself to be God' and demanding worship (verse 4). But in the meantime something is restraining or holding back the appearance of this horrible figure, 'so that he may be revealed at the proper time' (verse 6). Interestingly, Paul describes this 're-strainer' both as a person (verse 7) and as a thing (verse 6).

This 'lawless one' will perform 'signs and wonders' by the power of Satan, thus deceiving many into following him (verses 9–10). But he will then be swept away by the Lord Jesus himself at his coming, destroyed 'by the breath [or Spirit] of his mouth' (verse 8).

Presumably, if Paul would tell us to keep expecting the second coming of Jesus, even though 1,950 years have elapsed, then he would also tell us to keep expecting this 'rebellion' and the coming of the lawless one, because the two 'comings' are closely connected here. But things may not be as simple as this. Rather a different picture appears, when we set his teaching here alongside Mark 13.

Jesus predicts a similar future. He looks ahead to the appearance of 'the abomination that causes desolation, standing where it does not belong' (Mark 13:14). This event will herald a time of dreadful distress and difficulty, sometimes called the 'great tribulation', marked also by 'false Christs and false prophets' who will deceive people by performing 'signs and miracles' (13:15–22). Then 'the Son of Man' will appear, sweeping this suffering aside and rescuing 'the elect' (13:24–27).

It looks as though we can connect these events with each other:

▶ The 'lawless one' in 2 Thessalonians 2 is the same as 'the abomination that causes desolation' in Mark 13.

▶ The 'rebellion' in 2 Thessalonians 2 is the same as the great tribulation in Mark 13.

▶ The coming of Jesus is the same as the coming of 'the Son of Man'.

The third point seems clear, and helps to establish the other two. But we need to think a little more about the first two points, and we must also ask whether Mark 13 helps us to know what Paul meant by 'the restrainer'.

The 'lawless one' and the 'abomination'

The strange phrase 'abomination of desolation' in Mark 13:14 comes in fact from Daniel 11:31, where it refers to a coming pagan king who will try to destroy Israel. He will 'desecrate the temple', abolishing the sacrifices there (11:31), and then 'exalt and magnify himself above every god' (11:36). Paul says the same about 'the lawless one' here (verse 4), drawing on the language of Daniel 11:36.

In Jesus' day everyone believed that Daniel's prophecy had been fulfilled in the person of Antiochus IV Epiphanes, the king of Syria 175–163 BC. At that time Israel was part of the Syrian kingdom, and in 168 BC Antiochus decided to standardize religion throughout his kingdom, which meant abolishing Judaism and making all his subjects worship the Greek gods. He believed that he was an incarnation of the Greek god Zeus, and claimed this by his surname 'Epiphanes' which means 'appearing on earth'. He called himself simply 'god' on his coins. So he banned the daily sacrifices in worship of the God of Israel, and set up a statue of Zeus over the altar in the temple in Jerusalem. The Jews rebelled against Antiochus, and after a three-year guerrilla war his power over Israel was broken and the sacrifices were restored.

So when Jesus quotes Daniel and turns it into a prophecy again, he is saying that its significance wasn't exhausted by Antiochus Epiphanes. The temple is to be desecrated again. In fact, Jesus has just predicted its destruction (Mark 13:2), and we should probably connect the two. He expected the temple to be violated and destroyed.

By using the language of Daniel 11, and referring to the temple, Paul is basically saying the same thing about 'the lawless one'. Another Antiochus-like figure is to appear, but this time even worse – because he will perform 'signs and

147

wonders' to deceive people. Paul attaches Jesus' prophecy of the 'false Christs' who perform miracles (Mark 13:22) directly to this 'lawless one'.

How should we apply all this to ourselves? We will save this question until we have thought through some of the other puzzles in this passage.

Questions

1. Why was the temple so important, and its destruction so significant? What did its destruction mean, and what does it mean for us today? (Some notes on this are provided below.)
2. Who could this 'lawless one' be? Can you think of any other Antiochus-like figures, either in the past or in the world today? Through the centuries various options have been suggested: Roman emperors who demanded to be worshipped as gods; the popes or the papacy generally; tyrannical rulers like Ghengis Khan or Hitler; atheist systems like Marxism or communism; false religions that deceive people. Which of these fit? Some? Or none?
3. Does this passage make you afraid? Be honest about your feelings. What would Paul say to you about them?

The end of the temple?

At the time of writing 2 Thessalonians, the temple in Jerusalem was the centre of the Jewish world. Jews all around the Mediterranean sent their 'temple tax' every year, and the Roman authorities gave special permission for the collection and transport of this large amount of money. As a result, the temple was very wealthy, and beautifully adorned, a fitting symbol of the special covenant relationship between Israel and her God. Jews believed that

God had committed himself to preserve and prosper Jerusalem, as the place where he had chosen to 'put his Name there' (see Deuteronomy 12:5–7; Psalms 46 and 48).

But in AD 70, as Jesus predicted, the temple was completely destroyed by the Romans. Only the famous Western Wall (sometimes called the Wailing Wall) remains.

Inevitably, its destruction caused great heart-searching among Jews. How has God allowed this to happen? Does this mean the end of his special relationship with Israel? Should we seek to rebuild the temple, or does this show that God does not want temple worship any more? Was this a punishment for sin? If so, whose? Christian Jews were caught up in these questions also, although they had a different perspective on it, because Jesus had predicted the destruction of the temple, and given them a way to understand it. 'Don't you know that you yourselves are God's temple?' Paul asks the Corinthians (1 Corinthians 3:16). Because of Jesus, the temple has already been rebuilt. In fact, says John, it was rebuilt when Jesus rose from the dead, for his body is the temple, the 'place' where God's name dwells, and we become the temple as we are joined to him. See John 2:19–22; 4:21–24; 1 Corinthians 3:16–17; Ephesians 2:19–22; Hebrews 3:1–6; 1 Peter 2:4–5.

This gave Christian Jews a great message of hope and comfort for their fellow-Jews in those dark days following the sack of Jerusalem by Rome.

2 Thessalonians 2:3b–12

And also ... the 'rebellion' and the 'restrainer'

Paul reminds the Thessalonians (and us) of the sufferings to come and the task they (and we) must fulfil.

We carry on with the questions we started tackling in the last section.

The 'rebellion' and the great tribulation

If Paul was picking up Jesus' teaching about 'the abomination of desolation', and drawing further on Daniel 11 in his teaching about 'the lawless one', then it is likely that 'the rebellion' is his description of the coming tribulation predicted by Jesus in Mark 13:15–22. For this tribulation, Jesus said, would occur with the appearance of the 'abomination' in the temple.

This is important, for the older translations use the expression 'falling away' here, rather than 'rebellion', suggesting that Paul is thinking of a loss of faith by the church, rather than a rebellion by the world. Following this idea, the New American Standard Bible translates it 'apostasy'.

But it seems unlikely that Paul is thinking of a terrible time of faithlessness in the church. His Greek word (*apostasia*) means 'revolt, rejection of authority, disorder'. It is sometimes used of rebellion by God's people against God, but it doesn't necessarily mean this. Paul has in mind a period of dreadful disorder and rebellion against God, associated with the appearance of 'the lawless one' in the temple.

Jesus' prophecy was fulfilled in the Jewish War of AD 67–73. Led by various Zealot hotheads, the Jews rebelled against Roman rule, and provoked a terrible backlash. Jerusalem was attacked and besieged by the Romans; the Zealots holed up in the temple and desecrated it by fearful atrocities. Finally, amid appalling suffering and loss of life, the city was captured and the temple destroyed completely.

Jesus said that the suffering associated with 'the abomination of desolation' would be 'unequalled from the beginning, when God created the world, until now' (Mark 13:19). And certainly the suffering described by the Jewish historian Josephus (who was present throughout the war) is truly dreadful. Thousands upon thousands lost their lives, killed by the Romans, or by the Zealots, or by famine, and many, many more were made homeless. The Sadducees and all the ruling families were wiped out completely. Many Jews, like those at Masada, the last fortress to fall to the Romans, committed suicide rather than fall into their hands.

Paul's word *apostasia* is a good one to summarize all of this. There was no single 'lawless one' at that time, but 'lawlessness' reigned supreme through the appalling catalogue of crime described by Josephus. But if we see a fulfilment of Paul's, and Jesus', prophecy in the events of the Jewish War, we are left with the vital question: what about the coming of the Son of Man? Jesus expected it 'immediately after the distress [or tribulation] of those days' (Matthew 24:29), and clearly Paul shared this expectation (see verse 8). We will come back to this question in the next section.

What is the restrainer?

Paul reminds the Thessalonians that he had pointed to a factor, or person, *holding back* the appearance of 'the lawless one' until 'the proper time' (verses 6–7). What can this be? In my researches I have come across seven different things which have been suggested here: the main ones being God, the devil, Paul himself, the Roman empire, and the preaching of the gospel. How can we decide?

Again Mark 13 helps. Before describing the 'abomination of desolation', Jesus tells his disciples that they will hear of wars, but 'the end is still to come' (13:7), because they must be his 'witnesses' or bear testimony before governors and kings for his sake (13:9). 'The gospel must first be preached to all nations' (13:10). In this testimony, the Holy Spirit will be alongside them, giving them the words to say when they stand before a hostile world (13:11). But, he says, when they see 'the abomination of desolation', they must not stand, but flee (13:14).

There's our 'restrainer' – which is both a thing and a person. The end cannot come until the gospel has been preached worldwide, and the Holy Spirit has finished his ministry of standing alongside the church, enabling our testimony. We realize now why Paul slipped in that comment about his 'testimony' to the Thessalonians in 1:10, where he uses the same word as in Mark 13:9. He was fulfilling Jesus' call, relying on the Holy Spirit (see 1 Corinthians 2:13), bearing testimony to all the world (see Colossians 1:5–6). There will come a point, he says, when that task is complete, this 'restrainer' will be taken away (verse 7), and then 'the lawless one will be revealed'.

So far, so good. But there are puzzles here. The gospel had not been preached to all the world before AD 70, when Jesus' prophecy was fulfilled and the temple was destroyed. And even though there was dreadful suffering and 'lawlessness' then, he (the 'Son of Man') did not return. We will tackle these puzzles next.

Questions

1. How much of the world has heard the gospel? Why not get one of the group to research this question, perhaps using Patrick Johnstone's *Operation World* (Operation Mobilisation, 1993).
2. In what ways do you think the preaching of the gospel 'restrains' evil in our world?
3. The Thessalonians were already experiencing the

sufferings predicted by Jesus. No wonder Paul prayed that their love would not grow cold (Matthew 24:12; 1 Thessalonians 4:9–10; 2 Thessalonians 3:5)! But the same experience is faced by many Christians today. Why does God not intervene on their behalf? What is the purpose of suffering? (See Mark 4:13–20; 2 Corinthians 4:7–18.)

2 Thessalonians 2:3b–12

And then ... the coming of Jesus in splendour

Paul answers some of our questions about the coming of the 'lawless one' and the coming of Jesus.

In verse 8 it seems that no time elapses between the revealing of the lawless one, and the coming of Jesus to destroy him. Paul seems to picture it like this:

- The mystery or 'secret power' of 'lawlessness' is deeply at work in the world at the moment (verse 7).

- But the true horror, the real heart, of 'lawlessness' cannot be manifested, because

- the gospel is being preached and the Holy Spirit is active to support our testimony.

- But at some point this restraint will be taken away (verse 7b). The moment will come when the gospel has been fully preached, and the Spirit will no longer oppose evil through that preaching.

- At that moment there will be nothing to stop a ghastly, final manifestation of evil, wielding the power of the devil himself (verse 9). (John seems to picture the same thing in Revelation 20:7–8: Satan is no longer bound, but released to deceive the nations.)

▶ But then the Spirit will reappear as 'the Spirit of his mouth' – the mouth of the Lord Jesus, speaking at his coming in conquering judgment on all who reject his rule (verse 8: the word 'breath' is literally 'Spirit').

What a powerful picture! But Paul leaves us with a puzzle, for it looks as though he expected all this to take place in connection with the destruction of the temple in Jerusalem – following Jesus' teaching on this. He wasn't to know that the temple would be destroyed within twenty years of writing 2 Thessalonians. He himself died in about AD 65, just before the Jewish War started. Our question is: what would he have said, if he had lived to see the temple destroyed without the coming of Jesus at the same time? In fact, what would he say about 1,930 years of continuing human history, after that dreadful event?

I believe he would say this:

How merciful of God, to allow so much time for the preaching of the gospel and for repentance! Of course the Son of Man could not come in AD 70 – the gospel had not yet been preached throughout the world, as Jesus said it must. So the prophecy is being fulfilled in a way I did not expect. But don't be shaken in mind – fulfilment is certain, as soon as the gospel is fully proclaimed.

A distant closeness

Some 'double stars' are really double: two stars orbiting around each other. But the famous double star in the Plough or Great Bear (visible all year in the northern hemisphere) only *looks* double. The two stars are separated by many light-years, but are on almost the same line of sight from the Earth. Both Paul, and we, discover that the 'abomination' and the coming of the Son of Man are in fact apparent double stars. They looked as though they revolved around each other, but in fact we must cross a wide space between them – the whole 'gospel age'.

So let's ask Paul another question: Do you think that what you wrote about 'the man of lawlessness' setting himself up in the temple was completely fulfilled in the events of AD 67–70 in Jerusalem? Or should we expect further fulfilment? I think Paul would say:

Jesus' prophecy of the 'abomination of desolation' was certainly fulfilled then, and the awful corruption of the temple in AD 67–70 certainly matches what I had in mind. But the 'mystery of lawlessness' is always at work. The gospel is always opposed. And I think you could well expect some great manifestation of evil when the gospel age ends, immediately before the Lord Jesus comes in glory. For God's world is also his temple, you know. He inhabits his universe, but the powers try to take it over.

What form might this final rebellion take? It is very hard to say. But we see the pattern in Antiochus Epiphanes: a power which demands total loyalty, and forbids the public worship and recognition of Jesus. It's already to be seen, in many places.

This evil power feeds upon the rejection of the gospel. In verses 9–10 Paul explains that this power will be able to deceive people 'because they refused to love the truth and so be saved'. This implies that they have already heard the truth, and rejected it. Consequently they are open to being deceived by the power of 'lawlessness'. Having rejected the truth, deception is the only possibility left!

So we see again that the worldwide preaching of the gospel is the essential precondition for the coming of 'the lawless one'. It is only when people have decisively rejected the gospel that verses 11–12 can be true of them ('God sends them a powerful delusion so that they will believe the lie …'). God isn't acting to stop people from seeing the truth – perish the thought. No: this is what happens, inevitably, to people who have already seen the truth, and rejected it. Ultimately, God confirms them in the rejection they have chosen, by presenting them with a dreadful deception, into which they will of course fall.

Questions

1. When can we decide that someone, or some group of people, has finally rejected the gospel? Can we ever decide this?
2. Fill in the rest of the sentence: 'The worldwide preaching of the gospel will be finished when ...' See Romans 15:19: what does 'fully proclaimed' mean? Do you think it will be possible to see the moment of 'full proclamation' approaching?
3. Think of followers of another religion near you. They probably have some awareness of Christianity, but how accurate is it? Can they be said to have rejected Christ without a clear understanding of him? How can you graciously communicate with them?

Is 'the man of lawlessness' the same as the antichrist?

Neither Paul here, nor Jesus in Mark 13 and Matthew 24, uses the expression 'antichrist', and so I have not mentioned 'the antichrist' in the discussion above. But many make the connection between 'the man of lawlessness' here and 'the antichrist' as described in 1 John 2:18, 22; 4:3 and 2 John 7.

Who or what is this 'antichrist'? Just as the coming of the 'man of lawlessness' is foreshadowed by the presence of 'the secret power of lawlessness' in the world around us now (see 2 Thessalonians 2:6–8), so also the 'antichrist' is a definite future figure (1 John 2:18), but 'the spirit of antichrist ... is already in the world' (1 John 4:3). John goes so far as to say that 'many deceivers who do not acknowledge Jesus Christ as coming in the flesh have gone out into the world. *Any such person* is the deceiver and the antichrist. Watch out ...' (2 John 7–8).

In a similar way, Jesus predicts 'false Christs and false prophets' who deceive people by performing signs and miracles (Mark 13:22). These will appear at the time of the 'abomination of desolation'. But he also predicts that 'false prophets ... will deceive many' in the near future, before the time of the 'abomination' (Matthew 24:11).

And again, also painting a similar picture, John in Revelation foresees the coming of two beasts. One of these claims divine status and worship (Revelation 13:6–8 – like the 'man of lawlessness' in 2 Thessalonians 2:4), while the other performs signs to deceive people (Revelation 13:13–14) – like the 'man of lawlessness' in 2 Thessalonians 2:9–10. But as he describes these beasts, we realize that their effect and their power are already visible in the world around. They, too, are not just a future expectation. John's readers would particularly have identified these beasts in the Roman Empire, whose power was enforced by the imperial cult: everyone was expected to worship the goddess 'Rome', or the current emperor, in specially built temples. Anyone who failed to join in could be accused of disloyalty to Rome, the great saviour-state.

So whether we are thinking of the beasts, or the false christs or prophets, or the antichrist, or the man of lawlessness, the pattern is the same: a future figure whose power, spirit, and especially *deception* are experienced already, in the persecution of the church and in opposition to Jesus, the true Saviour. In fact the emphasis seems to fall on the present experience, rather than on the future coming, especially in the case of the antichrist and the beasts.

Commenting on 2 Thessalonians 2 in 1550, the great reformer John Calvin emphasized this present-tense aspect, for he saw the papacy of the Roman Catholic Church as 'the antichrist'. He saw the popes of that time as secular rulers, rather than spiritual leaders, wielding great power in opposition to the true gospel of Jesus Christ, while proclaiming themselves God's representatives on earth (compare 2 Thessalonians 2:4). But now, he said, this power is already being overthrown by the breath of Jesus' mouth (2 Thessalonians 2:8), because the true gospel is being proclaimed and Rome's influence is being undermined. When Jesus comes, he will complete the process of judgment which he has already begun. 'In the meantime, Christ will scatter the darkness in which Antichrist will reign by the rays which he will emit before his coming, just as the sun, before becoming visible to us, chases away the darkness of the night with its bright light.'

I think that Calvin shows us the right approach here. Asked, 'Who is the antichrist?', he didn't start speculating about what this future figure would look like. Taking his lead from 2 John 7, he asked, 'Where, in the world today, do we see great deception, great self-exaltation, great persecution of the church of Christ?' That's antichrist! Even if such horrors increase to a climax just before Jesus comes, we have to face the world as it is, and stand for Jesus now, in that world. Calvin did it in his day, by speaking out bravely against the abuses of the church as he knew it, and on behalf of the clear teaching of Scripture.

Where is the antichrist today, at the start of a new millennium? Ask the same three questions (great deception, self-exaltation and persecution), and the answers quickly emerge.

Does God deceive people?

Paul's words in 2 Thessalonians 2:11–12 seem a bit horrifying: 'God sends them a powerful delusion so that they will believe the lie and so that [they] will all be condemned.' Wow! Is he really saying that God deceives people, prevents them from seeing and accepting the truth, with the intention that they will be 'condemned'? This seems quite contrary to what Paul says about God elsewhere, 'who wants all … to be saved and to come to a knowledge of the truth' (1 Timothy 2:4).

This is one of those cases where a verse can give a completely false impression, when it's extracted from its context and read on its own. There are three vital points to make about this.

First, *we are responsible for our own deception*. I tried to bring this out in the comment above. The people about whom Paul is writing in verses 11–12 have already heard 'the truth', the gospel, and have rejected it. The Bible never lets us human beings off the hook, however much we might want to shuffle the blame off on to our family, our background, our environment, or God. If we reject the truth, we choose deception for ourselves.

Secondly, *Satan is the deceiver, not God*. 'When he lies,' said Jesus about the devil, 'he speaks his native language, for he is a liar and the father of lies' (John 8:44). Here in 2 Thessalonians 2 it is 'the work of Satan' which is revealed in these 'lying signs' and 'in all deception of wickedness' (verses 9–10, literal translations). According to Paul here, God is acting to restrain this power to deceive, through the preaching of the gospel. God will not promote the work of Satan.

Thirdly, however, *God is in charge of all that happens in his world*. Paul reflects this belief in verse 11. The deception is Satan's, but 'God sends' it, because nothing happens in his world outside his control or will.

There is a great mystery here, which we can't fully understand. But the mystery attaches to the reasons for the fact, rather than to the fact itself. Finally, the Bible gives no answer to the mysterious question: *why* does God allow his world to be filled with lying, deception, murder and wickedness – so much so that he himself had to take human flesh in order to rescue us? But the Bible gives a very clear answer to the question: does God rule over everything that happens in his world, so that nothing takes him by surprise? The answer is Yes! Yes! He rules without compromise, and works out his ultimate purpose of redemption even through the wickedness and lies of Satan. The cross of Jesus is the ultimate proof of this.

8

BELONGING TO JESUS IN THE MEANTIME

2 Thessalonians 2:13 – 3:5

Stop and look: what is happening in 2:13 – 3:5?

There's a bit of a break in the letter at 3:1, where Paul begins to round things off with 'Finally, brothers ...' But actually there is no break in thought there. This next section of the letter carries on by summarizing 'life in the meantime': what are the 'rules of engagement' for living in this world before Jesus comes again?

The whole section has a careful structure, which often happens with Paul's writing. We can set it out like this:

A Confidence in God (2:13–14)
  B Concern for the Thessalonians' obedience (2:15)
    C Prayer for their strengthening (2:16–17)
      D Prayer for the spread of the gospel (3:1–2)
A¹ Confidence in God (3:3)
  B¹ Concern for the Thessalonians' obedience (3:4)
    C¹ Prayer for their strengthening (3:5)

You notice how A and A¹, B and B¹ and C and C¹ match each other, and group around D which is introduced by Paul's emphatic 'Finally, brothers'. It's not surprising that, at the heart of 'Belonging to Jesus in the meantime', there lies the spreading of the gospel. As we saw above, it's highly likely that the worldwide preaching of the gospel is the 'restraining power' to which Paul refers in 2:6–7.

If we put Paul on the spot and pinned him down, he would say to us: there is no more important calling, and no more vital task, for the church of Jesus Christ than spreading 'the message of the Lord' (3:1), that is, the message about the Lord Jesus. This is the theme that runs through this whole section, as we will see.

2 Thessalonians 2:13–14

Being 'firstfruits' for him

There is so much to frighten us in this world. But Paul gives us solid grounds for confidence, and an end to fear.

 The last four verses (2:9–12) have been very sombre. They picture a world in which devilish powers deceive people and ruin their lives (verse 9), in which the gospel is rejected and evil prevails (verse 10), in which God allows people to sink into the mess they make of their lives (verse 11), and in which the first casualty is truth, and people delight in wickedness (verse 12).

Familiar? It sounds just like an episode from a soap opera! That's the world we live in – a frightening, uncertain, hostile place. A dark world, haunted by the ghosts of wickedness past, wracked by the news of a violent present, oppressed by fears of horrors to come, resting uneasily on fault-lines through which the powers of hell grumble and press, and threaten to burst upward with devastation and destruction. Misery is our lot, and more misery our destination. For most people, the new millennium holds no prospect of hope or a new start.

Unless ... unless you are 'loved by the Lord' (verse 13): the Lord Jesus, that is. To be loved by him, in the midst of all that danger and misery, is to walk secure through the minefield, to fall safe into a parent's arms, to lie down beside still waters.

Verse 13 begins with an emphatic 'But we'. In contrast to all the misery and uncertainty around, we Christians have a different story to tell. But Paul doesn't just rejoice for himself. Most unusually, he now repeats his thanksgiving from the beginning of the letter (1:3), rejoicing that his beloved Thessalonians are secure within this threatening world.

What is this confidence, and on what does it rest? We can point to three factors here.

In the past – 'called'

The emphatic 'we' at the beginning of verse 13 is matched by another in verse 14, 'He called you to this through *our* gospel.' The ground for Paul's thanksgiving is that, when he preached the gospel in Thessalonica, God 'called' them through it – that is, they were 'saved through the sanctifying work of the Spirit and through belief in the truth' (verse 13). Paul knows that God has been at work in their lives, because they believed the message, and he saw the Holy Spirit changing and 'sanctifying' them. This is the 'restrainer' at work – the gospel exercising its power to push back evil and rescue lives.

See the comments about God's 'call' above (p. 73): it's like being called up or conscripted into God's army. Not a 'call' you can turn down! That's how the Thessalonians experienced it. It transformed them. Looking at them, Paul knew that God had chosen them, because of the way they believed the gospel and showed supernatural joy under immediate persecution (1 Thessalonians 1:4–7).

That's the work of the Spirit! There's a deliberate contrast between verses 12b and 13b: the world around does not believe the truth, and instead delights in wickedness; but the Thessalonians have believed the truth, and have been touched by the holiness of the Holy Spirit. The work of the Holy Spirit, for Paul, is always obvious.

In the present – 'chosen'

Because of what happened to them in the past, they can now call themselves 'loved by the Lord', 'chosen as first-fruits'. (NIV has 'from the beginning' instead of 'as firstfruits' – there's a note about this below.) To know, deep in our hearts, that we are loved is a most wonderful thing –

an experience denied to so many in our world today. All who believe the gospel come into this immediate awareness that they are loved by the Christ who died for them. Sometimes this sense of being loved is hard to acquire, or hard to keep, because of family background and experience. But it is part of the Christian's birthright.

'Chosen as firstfruits' adds another note. God has chosen them not just for their own sake, but for the sake of those around them in Thessalonica. The 'firstfruits' were the first bit of the harvest, specially belonging to God and offered to him in thankfulness for the whole harvest about to be gathered (see Exodus 23:16, 19; 34:26). The church in Thessalonica is small, persecuted, weak, despised – but they are *only the firstfruits* of God's harvest in that city. Being 'chosen' means being strategically placed for spreading the Good News and reaping the harvest.

In the future – 'sharing glory'

These two verses definitely move to a climax in verse 14b. God's ultimate purpose and plan, in which he will not fail, is 'that you might share in the glory of our Lord Jesus Christ'. 'Obtain' would be a better translation than 'share in'. Paul uses the same rather striking word in 1 Thessalonians 5:9: 'God did not appoint us to suffer wrath but to receive [or obtain] salvation through our Lord Jesus Christ.'

Earlier, he pictured the Thessalonians being caught up into the glory of Jesus, joining his triumphal procession at his return (1:10, 12). But now they *obtain* the glory of Jesus, as if it were their own possession. Jesus does not just permit them to carry the crown jewels in the procession, but gives them crowns of their own, and tells them to rule on his behalf (see Romans 5:17). This is an amazing thought.

Questions

1. Many Christians struggle with a deep sense of guilt and unworthiness. What causes this? Is it good or bad?

2. Think about the evangelistic strategy of your church. How are you planning to reap God's harvest in your town or area?
3. Can you compose a modern parable to illustrate some of the truths in these verses – the things that give total security in the midst of a dark and dangerous world?

'From the beginning' or 'as firstfruits'?

Most modern translations, including NIV, have 'from the beginning' in verse 13, but the New Revised Standard Version has 'God chose you as the first fruits for salvation'. The Good News Bible has something similar, and NIV suggests a similar alternative in a footnote in most editions. This is an example of a variation in the early Greek manuscripts which actually makes quite a difference to the meaning.

I have followed the NRSV rather than the NIV in the comments above, because I'm convinced that 'as firstfruits' is more likely to have been what Paul wrote. This is also the view of the latest edition of the Greek New Testament. Strange to say, the difference between the two is only one letter in the Greek, so it was a mistake that could easily have been made by an early scribe. The challenge for scholars, in a case like this, is threefold:

1 They must assess the manuscript evidence: does this give any clues as to which came first? In this case, important early manuscripts appear on both sides and the decision is balanced.
2 They must ask which of the two is more likely to have been corrupted by scribes. In this case, 'chosen from the beginning' is such a standard phrase that, if this were the original, it is hard to see how it could have been corrupted to 'as firstfruits'. But 'as firstfruits' is unusual

and could well have been changed to 'from the beginning'.

3 They must ask which fits Paul's argument better. Here, either fits without difficulty but 'as firstfruits' matches Paul's interest in the preaching of the gospel in this passage.

Translators sometimes have difficult choices to make when they face little points like this in the Bible. Because the texts of the New Testament were copied by hand for over 1,400 years until the invention of printing, there was plenty of time for scribal errors to appear. So now painstaking detective work is needed, to recover the original text at places where the manuscripts differ from each other. But it is important to say that no vital doctrine or element of the message of the New Testament is in any way undermined by a textual problem of this sort.

And it is also important to bear in mind that we have far more manuscripts of the New Testament, and far greater certainty about the original text, than for any other work of similar age. For instance, the Roman historian Tacitus' famous *Annals of Imperial Rome*, which tells the story (among other things) of Nero and his persecution of the Christians, is preserved only in a single eighth-century manuscript. There are over 5,000 manuscripts of all or part of the New Testament.

The vast majority of such variations concern only details, like this one. Most of them are too insignificant to mention. For instance, some early manuscripts have 'he called us' rather than 'he called you' in verse 14. But the three questions outlined above make it clear that 'you' is original, and the translators have not put a footnote about it.

2 Thessalonians 2:15–17

Standing for him

**Paul urges the Thessalonians to stand firm for the Lord in a
hostile society, and prays for the things they need, in
order to do that.**

'So then, brothers' (verse 15): 'So then'
is the introduction Paul uses when he is
drawing conclusions from what has
gone before (see *e.g.* Romans 8:12; 14:19;
Ephesians 2:19; 1 Thessalonians 5:6). Here it's the practical
consequences of all that he has written in the chapter so far,
looking back to 2:2 where he expressed his concern that the
Thessalonians were being shaken (NIV, 'unsettled'). He feels
that he has given them many reasons not to be 'shaken', but
rather to 'stand firm'. He has shown them that the day of
the Lord has not come, and why. He has reminded them of
God's purpose of salvation for them. So now he tells them
what their response should be.

Hold to the traditions

Paul still has Jesus' teaching in Mark 13 running through his
mind, I believe. The word for 'stand firm' is the same as the
word in Mark 13:9, 'you will *stand* before governors and
kings as witnesses ...' So by telling them to 'stand firm',
Paul doesn't want them to retreat into defensiveness, trying
to remain inconspicuous while making sure that all their
doctrines are present and correct. He has something much
more adventurous and outward-looking in mind. As Jesus
foresaw, they face hostile authorities (see Acts 17:1–9), and
they must be ready to 'stand firm' in their witness.

Essential to 'standing firm' is 'holding on'. Like trekkers

crossing a swollen river, they need something to hold on to, or they will be swept away. Those false ideas about the day of the Lord will undermine their testimony, dislodge their footing, and lead to disaster. But if they will 'hold to the teachings we passed on to you' then they will be able to stand.

Paul is thinking of the teaching he gave them, of which he has just reminded them (see 2:5). He has taught them 'by word of mouth' when with them, and also 'by letter' (thinking probably of both 1 and 2 Thessalonians). But in fact he uses the word 'traditions', rather than 'teachings' (NIV margin is better), as if to remind them of what we have noticed – that this teaching comes not just with his own authority, but with the authority of the Lord Jesus himself.

This is so important! In a multicultural world it is much easier to talk about 'God' than about 'Jesus'. A belief in 'God' we share with many other religious people, and it is tempting to feel that this gives us quite a lot of common ground with them. And to some extent this is true. But we are not commissioned to talk about 'God', but about *Jesus*: and Jesus divides us off, makes us different – and gives us a message. The Jews in Thessalonica would never have taken offence at Paul if he had just talked about 'God'. But he came faithfully to bear 'testimony' (2 Thessalonians 1:10; Mark 13:9) about Jesus, and eventually to pass on the traditions of *his* teaching to the new church there. Are we ready to bear the stigma of clear, public association with the name of Jesus, speaking for *him* rather than just for 'God'?

Paul knows that they cannot do this in their own strength, and so he bursts into prayer for them (verses 16–17) – the first of three short prayers in the last part of the letter (see also 3:5, 3:16). His prayer has three parts:

1 *To whom?* He directs his prayer primarily to 'our Lord Jesus Christ himself': distinctively Christian prayer, to strengthen distinctively Christian testimony. We know God as 'our Father' only because of Jesus. Otherwise he is just a distant deity, an Ultimate Cause or Supreme Force or Absolute Ground, but not a Father.

2 *Why?* Verse 16b ('who loved us ...') probably attaches both to Jesus and to the Father – combined here under a single 'who'. Paul prays because this God, who is God-in-Christ, is the Giver of grace, encouragement and hope. Only this God can give these things, the God who has shown his love for us by giving us his Son, precisely so that we may have hope of eternal life and be encouraged that we have a future. This God alone can answer Paul's prayer. Otherwise, 'encouragement' and 'hope' in the face of this horrible world are mere wishful thinking.

3 *For what?* Paul prays that this God will do what he alone can do: 'encourage your hearts and strengthen you in every good deed and word'. Once again, we see Paul's prescription for a persecuted church: it is not to retreat from sight, to keep off the streets and safe in the fellowship, but to do, and to speak, in the name of Jesus. This will be difficult, and they must be wise about *how* they do it, but God will surely encourage and strengthen them for it.

Questions

1. Imagine the situation in some Muslim countries, where direct witness to Muslims is forbidden by law. How do you think Christians in those circumstances can be 'encouraged and strengthened in every good deed and word'? What do you think Paul would tell them to do? Turn your thoughts into prayer, as Paul did.

2. Most western societies are now consciously pluralistic – that is, all religions are meant to coexist in mutual respect and tolerance, with none being privileged over the others. This is true even of societies which have been traditionally 'Christian'. Is this pluralism a good thing, or not? How may Christians witness effectively within religious pluralism?

3. What are 'good deeds and words'? What are the kinds of things for which you think the Lord Jesus would want to strengthen and encourage you?

2 Thessalonians 3:1–2

Praying harvesters for him

Prayer is front-line engagement in the battle for world-wide evangelization.

 Having prayed for them (2:16–17), Paul now asks the Thessalonians to pray for him and his companions. As we noticed above, this request for prayer is right at the heart of this section of the letter, emphatic and clear. And it fits with Paul's emphasis on the spreading of the gospel. If the worldwide preaching of the gospel (a) holds back lawlessness (2:7), and (b) prepares the way for the Lord's coming (2:8), then Paul has already given us two very good reasons to pray 'that the word of the Lord may run and be glorified' (verse 1, literal translation).

'The Lord' here is of course the Lord Jesus, although Paul is using the word *kyrios*, the regular Old Testament name for God himself. He refers to 'the Lord' four times in these verses (1, 3, 4, 5), and on each occasion is thinking of Jesus, rather than God. This becomes extra-clear in 3:6, where he talks to them sternly 'in the name of the Lord Jesus Christ'.

This application of the name 'Lord' to Jesus is all the more significant, because this strange thought of the word of the Lord 'running' is drawn from Psalm 147:15, where God himself is in mind: 'He sends his command to the earth; his word runs swiftly.' There, however, the running of his word throughout the world is not the preaching of a message, but the voice of creation: 'He spreads the snow like wool and scatters the frost like ashes. He hurls down hail like pebbles. Who can withstand his icy blast? He sends his word and melts them …' (Psalm 147:16–18).

But alongside this 'word' through the weather, 'He has

revealed his word to Jacob, his laws and decrees to Israel' (Psalm 147:19). The 'word' implicit in the voice of creation around us is declared explicitly and clearly, in 'words', to Israel.

We find just this parallel also in the famous Psalm 19, which begins with the voice of creation (verses 1–6), and then sets this alongside the voice of the law (verses 7–14).

In the first part, 'The heavens declare the glory of God' (verse 1), seen particularly in the sun which charges out of bed in the morning 'like a champion rejoicing to run his course' (verse 5). But if you really want to know how to live in this world which speaks so loudly of its Creator, then you must turn to 'the law of the LORD', which 'is perfect, reviving the soul … making wise the simple … giving joy to the heart' (verses 7–8).

The way out of the maze

This is the background to Paul's thinking about the worldwide preaching of the gospel. In Romans 10:18 he quotes from the first part of Psalm 19 to describe the worldwide spread of the gospel: 'their voice has gone out into all the earth, their words to the ends of the world!' Of course, in his day this had not yet fully happened – but this is his vision for it. The light of the gospel is like the light of the sun. They come from the same God, and the world is in darkness until they dawn. Without the gospel, it's like living in a maze. You know that it makes sense, and there's order, and arrangement, and reason all around you, because it's obvious – but you're still lost. You can find only dead ends. Then the gospel comes, and you discover the mind of the Creator, and begin to learn the map of the maze. Light dawns.

Only the gospel of Jesus, the *kyrios* (Lord), brings this light. For Paul, 'the word of the Lord' is now the gospel rather than the Old Testament law, about which Psalm 19 sings – not because they are in competition with each other, but because the gospel is the full story. The law gives you half the map of the maze.

So 'pray', he tells the Thessalonians: pray that this word will run round the world and 'be glorified' – that is, that its message will shine as it is embraced, believed and loved by people the world over. Probably Paul has in mind the crown given to the winner of a race. The gospel of Jesus is in competition with many rivals, all offering to explain the world and tell us how to live in it. But we must pray that the gospel will win this race for the hearts and minds of Earth's inhabitants.

That thought leads into verse 2. Everywhere it goes, the gospel is opposed. The 'secret power of lawlessness' is abroad. In 1 Thessalonians 2:13–16 Paul reminded the Thessalonians of how they received 'the word of God' when it came to them, but then immediately experienced dreadful opposition in line with the experience of Jesus himself, the subject of the message. Defeat was a real possibility. Paul was deeply anxious for them (1 Thessalonians 2:17 – 3:5). He must have prayed, over and over again, the prayer which he asks them to pray here: 'Lord, deliver them from those rebellious and evil people …' – the people who resist the light, who corner a bit of the maze for themselves and don't want to be told that it belongs to someone else.

The spread of the gospel is fuelled by the prayer of the church.

Questions

1. How does prayer work? Why do we need to pray, if God is in charge of his world and his church (remember 2:13–14)?
2. Review the way you, and/or your church, pray for missionaries. How can you improve it? Remember Matthew 9:35–38.
3. Who are the 'wicked and evil' people who oppose the gospel of Jesus today?

2 Thessalonians 3:3–5

Facing danger for him

We discover where we can find true confidence in the midst of the battle.

Just in case the Thessalonians might feel that Paul faced worse opposition than they did, Paul turns the thought of verse 2 around in verse 3. 'Pray for *us*' he asks – 'but I'm confident that the Lord will guard *you*!' We rightly pray for missionaries who, like Paul, go from us to other cultures to spread the gospel. But we all face the opposition to the gospel from which we pray that God will deliver them, and therefore we stand in danger, too.

'Evil men [= people]' in verse 2 becomes 'the evil one' in verse 3 – meaning, of course, the devil. Behind all opposition to the gospel there ultimately lies satanic power. That's why it's so dangerous. In western societies today the greatest opposition to the gospel comes, I believe, from the pleasure industry. With its 'feel-good' philosophy trumpeted through the mass media, and vast wealth applied to giving its devotees a good time, it has captured the mind of the masses and bred indifference towards God. Do you think that the apathy towards spiritual things which grips housing estates across the whole western world is somehow less serious, less satanic, than the outright opposition to Christ which animates Iranian Muslims or Chinese Communists? It's just a different sort of satanic deception aimed at stifling the voice of the gospel.

David Burnett tells the story of his visit to China, during which he asked some believers there, 'How are you managing to survive, under communism?'

They described the challenges of being the church in

China, and then returned the question: 'Tell us, how are you Christians in the West managing to survive under capitalism?'

The dangers are great. We can be swallowed by our enemies. But that's not the end of the story. There may be no faith in the world around (verse 2b), but 'The Lord is faithful, and he will strengthen and protect you from the evil one' (verse 3). Paul has lots of 'commands' to give them (verses 4, 6), but he has no confidence in *them*, that they will be able to do what he says. Rather, 'we have confidence *in the Lord*, that you are doing and will continue to do the things we command' (verse 4). He trusts *the Lord* for *their* obedience.

Paul probably has in mind the things he wrote in 2:13–14 about God's purpose and action towards them. Chosen by God, loved by the Lord Jesus, sanctified by the Spirit, called through the gospel, destined for glory ... what can withstand this line-up?

Direct your hearts

But Paul knows that he still needs to pray for them. And we too need the spiritual weapon of prayer if we are to battle against the enemies of our souls. Once again Paul puts his own prayer into words (verse 5). Having asked them to pray for him, he starts praying for them – thus giving them an example of the kind of praying for others that he has in mind.

What do they need, above all else, if they are to withstand the attacks of their enemies? In Thessalonica the enemies were very real, and the persecution direct and physical. But the real battle, Paul knew, was not 'out there', in the world where their enemies muster and plot, but 'in here', deep in their hearts. That's the real front line! And so he prays that the Lord will 'direct your hearts into the love of God and the endurance of Christ'. What does this mean? Three things:

First, *it means getting desire straight*. 'Direct your hearts' means 'sort out your emotions', 'create good desires', 'incline your inclinations'. We are creatures of emotion, and we are led by our desires. At the heart of 'sanctification', the process of becoming holy, is the redirection of our desires to their proper objects.

Secondly, *it means falling in love with the love of God.* Many people are 'in love with love' – that is, they want the experience the songs sing about, they want to be swept off their feet, madly in love, and bury themselves in that perfect relationship offering perfect fulfilment. We know it's an illusion. But it's a very potent illusion – because it's a corruption of true desire. We were made to love someone like that, and to enter a relationship which gives perfect fulfilment – with God!

And once we have tasted that kind of love with God, Paul knows, nothing else will satisfy. Every other love loses its potency, that is, its potential to distract us from the true love of our lives.

Thirdly, *it means wanting to share Jesus' experience.* People who fall in love want to share their lives with each other. They want to give themselves, and receive the other person. But we have a *suffering* Saviour. If we love him and want to 'receive' him into our lives, then we will want to share his sufferings, or his 'perseverance', as Paul puts it here. See Paul's expression of his own longing to do this, in Philippians 3:8–11. (See also 2 Corinthians 1:5; 4:11–12; 1 Peter 4:13–14.) Whatever we suffer as Christians will simply help us to enter into what he suffered as the Christ.

Paul's prayer here is very brief, and very profound.

Questions

1. In what ways might we, as Christians, fall prey to the deceptions of the pleasure industry?
2. How can we deepen our love for God? Is it something we simply have to ask him for, or can we deepen it ourselves?
3. Think of a practical way in which you (individually, or as a group) could encourage someone else, or another

group, in the way Paul encourages the Thessalonians here.

Patience

This word 'patience' (sometimes translated 'perseverance', as in verse 5, or 'endurance') is one of Paul's favourites. He has already used it in 2 Thessalonians 1:4, where he says that he boasted about the Thessalonians' 'perseverance'; and he uses it seventeen times altogether in his letters.

You might think that he would use it especially in connection with persecution. But he doesn't. For Paul, 'endurance/patience' is a central quality of the Christian life, whether we are undergoing persecution or not. What is it, exactly?

Surprisingly, Paul often talks about 'endurance' in connection with 'hope'. The two words appear together on seven occasions (*e.g.* Romans 5:3–5; 1 Thessalonians 1:3), and sometimes he uses 'endurance' where we might expect 'hope' to appear (*e.g.* Titus 2:2; 1 Timothy 6:11).

Romans 8:24–25 shows how he connects the two ideas of 'endurance' and 'hope'. We were saved in hope, he says – the hope which he has just described, that one day the whole world will be redeemed, and our bodies will be transformed, and we will enter full glory as God's children (Romans 8:18–23). 'But hope that is seen is no hope' (8:24) – in other words, hope as a quality arises because of a sense of distance between ourselves and something for which we long and expect to receive. In this sense, my daughter 'hopes' for her birthday party for at least six months before her birthday actually comes.

Paul goes on: 'But if we hope for what we do not yet have, we wait for it patiently' (8:25). In other words: if we are absolutely certain that we will one day enter God's yet invisible kingdom, then 'patience' grows as we wait. 'Hope' is something certain, for Paul. Not 'I hope for fine weather today' (never a certainty in Britain), but 'I hope for a birthday party!' (my daughter). And 'patience' is that *joyful* quality of enduring anticipation in the meantime, ready to travel the road, whatever it is, which will bring us to that goal.

Jesus showed this quality as he faced the cross, and indeed all the sufferings which preceded it. Hebrews 12:2 sums it up: '... who for the joy set before him endured the cross, scorning its shame, and sat down at the right hand of the throne of God'. So *endurance* is that quality of hope with which we face all the experiences, whatever they are, through which we need to pass, in order to come to the supreme joy of eternal life.

BUSINESS AS USUAL?

2 Thessalonians 3:6–18

In this last section of the letter Paul turns to the other issue which bothers him, that of lazy spongers in the Thessalonian church. Some Christians were just living off the generosity of others. Once again Paul's thoughts form themselves into a natural pattern:

A Instruction in Jesus' name (3:6a)
   B Action towards 'disorderly' brothers (3:6b)
      C^1 The tradition they reject: Paul's example (3:7–9)
      C^2 The tradition they reject: Paul's teaching (3:10)
   B^1 Who the 'disorderly' brothers are (3:11)
A^1 Instruction in Jesus' name (3:12)

Here too, as with the problem over the day of the Lord, Paul's concern is to remind the Thessalonians of what he showed them and taught them while with them. He is not the only Christian teacher, by any means, to wish that people could take things on board the first time they hear them.

Noticing this pattern helps us to see that 3:13–18 then forms the closing paragraph of the letter, although it is not printed like this in NIV.

Both paragraphs (3:6; 3:13) begin with Paul calling the Thessalonians 'brothers', and this reminds us of other paragraphs that begin in the same way (1:3; 2:1; 2:13; 2:15; 3:1). In addition, Paul refers to them as 'brothers' twice more (3:6; 3:15), making a total of nine, or once every 5.2 verses. So 2 Thessalonians confirms the special warmth that Paul seems to have felt for this church (see the statistics given above, p. 79). Of course, 'brothers' for Paul meant what 'brothers and sisters' means to us today.

This whole section gives us some priceless teaching on work and our attitudes towards it. In most countries the educational system is geared towards preparing young people for work, and from their earliest years they absorb the idea that somehow work is inevitable – whether they like it or not, they can't avoid it. Soon financial necessity underlines that point for them. But for many, work has little value in itself. Christians can easily have the same feeling, particularly if they are doing and experiencing really important things through their church, in the evenings and at weekends.

Churches encourage this downgrading of the value of work, by simply ignoring it. In his excellent book *Thank God it's Monday* (Scripture Union, 1997), Mark Greene reports a survey in which he discovered that over 50% of Christians have never heard a sermon on work, and over 70% have never received any careful Christian teaching on work. Yet 100% of Christians have a 'Monday to Friday', every week. Whether we are paid for it or not, we are all involved in work of some kind.

Paul was worried about the attitude of some Thessalonians towards work. I think he would have the same concerns about the church today.

2 Thessalonians 3:6–9

Having the right role model

Role models are vital, for young people particularly. Paul proposes himself as a role model for the Thessalonians in their attitude towards work.

The language of verse 6 is very strong. Paul didn't often issue 'commands' to his churches. As he says to Philemon, 'although in Christ I could be bold and order you to do what you ought to do, yet I appeal to you on the basis of love' (Philemon 8–9). Here, the word translated 'command' is not as tough as 'order' in Philemon 8, but even so, Paul is being unusually directive.

Yet we must notice two vital things:

▶ Paul is appealing to the authority of the Lord Jesus Christ. He does not issue this 'command' on his own authority.

▶ He gives *himself* as an example of what he wants them to do. He doesn't tell them to do anything he's not fully willing to do himself.

So what's the problem? Paul tells them 'to keep yourselves away from every brother who lives in a disorderly way, not following the tradition which you received from us' (verse 6, literal translation). NIV has 'idle' rather than 'disorderly', because that is what the problem turns out to be (verse 11): among the Thessalonians, some were refusing to work and, instead, were sponging off their wealthier 'brothers', presuming on their kindness and generosity.

This 'disorderly' behaviour has the same root cause as the problem over the day of the Lord: not living by the 'traditions' of the Lord Jesus. The two problems may be linked, for we can imagine people so caught up with 'heaven on earth' that they ignored the need to work for a living and provide for their families. But Paul calls this 'disorderly', not because it disrupts the 'normal' way of doing things in society, but because it disputes the teaching of Jesus, the 'tradition' Paul passed on.

What 'tradition' is this? Once again, Paul is probably still thinking of the teachings now preserved for us in Mark 13, Matthew 24 and Luke 21. Mark 13 and Matthew 24 both end with the parable of the watching servants (Mark 13:33–37; Matthew 24:45–51). Jesus tells his disciples to watch and warns them against getting drunk, just as Paul does in 1 Thessalonians 5:6–7. And Jesus pictures them as servants left in charge of the household by their master, who has given each his work to do until he returns (Mark 13:34).

This fits with the teaching earlier in Mark 13. When the final tribulation comes, says Jesus, then 'flee to the mountains. If you are on the roof of the house, don't go down to collect anything from inside. And if you are in the field, don't go back to get your coat ...' (Mark 13:14–16, my translation). The women would be working on the flat roof, washing or cooking, and the men would be working in the fields, stripped of their outer garments. Jesus assumes that, right up to these end-events, people will be working, even if they are also watching, praying and making ready for his return.

Paul had given some teaching on this in Thessalonica. In 1 Thessalonians 4:1–2 he reminds them of the instructions he gave them 'through the Lord Jesus' (see p. 69), and encourages them to obey 'more and more'. Then he specifies certain instructions in particular, including: 'Make it your ambition to lead a quiet life, to mind your own business and to work with your hands, just as we told you ...' (1 Thessalonians 4:11).

But they didn't. So Paul felt that he had the authority of Jesus to say with doubled emphasis: you *must work* quietly and steadily, while waiting for the Lord to come. This is remarkable, really. Although the world is dominated by 'the secret power of lawlessness' (2:7) and is in rebellion against God, Christians must not withdraw from it into a separate, closed, 'pure' society, but stay stuck into the workplace.

Why? Paul gives four reasons in this closing section of 2 Thessalonians (3:6–16). The first appears in these verses. We look at the other three in the last two studies.

We must work, because we must not 'burden' each other (verses 8–9)

Paul repeats here what he says a little more fully in 1 Thessalonians 2:9. Even though Jesus had given permission for missionaries to be supported by the people they went to (Matthew 10:9–10), Paul wanted to make the gospel 'free of charge' (see 1 Corinthians 9:14–18).

But he says that he acted like this in order to set an example for the whole church, not just for those called to be missionaries (verses 7, 9). The point is this: we have much more important things to share than money. 'Owe no one anything, except to love one another!' Paul tells the Romans (Romans 13:8, NRSV). When money and debt start to feature in the relationship between Christians, then our fellowship starts to skate on thin ice. It may look like an act of love to give to a fellow-believer, but ultimately money and debt distract from the real job of building one another up in Christ, loving one another in his name, encouraging one another to serve him. So easily, ingratitude and resentment displace love and fellowship. Even though he never received a penny except from spontaneous gifts, Paul was still accused of making money out of his churches (2 Corinthians 12:14–18). How much worse it would have been if he had asked them to follow Jesus' teaching and support him!

Questions

1. When did you last hear a sermon, or receive some teaching, on work? If in a group, share your 'Monday to

Friday' with each other, and the particular challenges you face as Christians at work (or out of work).
2. Should we never give money or other gifts to each other within a fellowship? How should we do it?
3. Unemployment is a terrible scourge, undermining people's self-confidence and sense of worth. What should or could churches be doing?

2 Thessalonians 3:10–12

Working and eating

**Paul gives two more reasons why we must work
while waiting for the Lord to return.**

It does seem strange. Surely: if the preaching of the gospel is the most vital thing of all, paving the way for the Lord's return, then doesn't it make sense for as many Christians as possible – why not all of us? – to be mobilized into evangelism, freed from the necessity to earn money? Why doesn't Paul encourage the Thessalonians to do this, perhaps exhorting the wealthier members of the church to take special responsibility for supporting the rest?

It sounds persuasive. And of course this is the argument behind the formation of missionary societies, of which there are thousands in the church today. But Paul doesn't tell the Thessalonians to form their own private missionary society, with some supporting others. He adds two more reasons why not.

We must work, because we all need to eat
(verses 10, 12)

Paul clearly felt very strongly about this. 'While we were with you, we kept giving you the rule "No work, no food!"' (my translation). The tense of the verb points to repeated teaching on this point. Why does he feel so strongly? Part of the answer is undoubtedly because Jesus said so (see below), but there's more to it than just that. He tells them that they each have an individual responsibility to feed and support themselves. Jesus tells them 'to settle down and earn the bread they eat' (verse 12).

We could ask Paul: 'But what about people who can't do that: the disabled, the long-term unemployed, the elderly?' It's important to remember the situation he was writing to. He has in mind people who are well able to work, but who have decided not to, probably for 'spiritual' reasons, and who as a result have become dependent on others for their 'bread'. No! he says. If we are able to work, we must, because work is the way it works in our world. We are physical beings, living in a physical world, in which 'by the sweat of your brow you shall eat your food until you return to the ground' (Genesis 3:19).

Work, whatever it is, is part of the rhythm of life. It's part of what it means to be human. God is a worker, and has designed the world to reflect his own pattern of work and rest (Genesis 2:1–3). In all sorts of work, however 'unspiritual' or even menial, we can be like him, expressing his rhythm of creation and rest. Ultimately, we work because we can't divide life into separate compartments, 'spiritual' and 'worldly'. God made the world, and we can know him as we add a column of figures, lay a row of bricks, change a nappy, clean a floor, win a contract.

Probably verse 10 is aimed as much at the wealthy Thessalonians as at the spongers. Paul is saying to them: 'Don't go along with this freeloading! If people are simply messing around, being busybodies rather than busy (verse 11), then resist their cries for help. No work, no food!'

We can see now why Paul was so keen to provide for

himself, even though he had the greatest possible reason to claim support from his churches. He had a very strong theology of work. We need it too. Incidentally, verse 8a probably doesn't mean that Paul never accepted hospitality from anyone, or always insisted on paying for the meal. It means he never depended on others for his food and support (compare 1 Thessalonians 4:12). He gratefully received gifts if they came – see Philippians 4:16–20.

We must work, because Jesus said so (verse 12)

Some people think that 'in the Lord Jesus Christ' means just that Jesus is involved in the situation, and cares about it. But probably Paul is appealing directly to Jesus' authority here, and is thinking of specific teachings of Jesus himself. There is no verse in the gospels in which Jesus says, 'Settle down and earn the bread you eat', but as we saw above, he pictures the disciples as servants doing their work patiently, while waiting for their Lord to return.

We could also point to the way in which Jesus draws many of his parables from the working world. Whether it's a housewife sweeping the house (Luke 15:8–10) or making bread (Matthew 13:33), or a farmer sowing (Mark 4:3–9) or reaping (Matthew 13:24–30), or a fisherman casting his nets (Matthew 13:47–50), or a shepherd (Luke 15:3–7), or a market-gardener (Luke 13:6–9), or an estate manager (Luke 16:1–9), or a builder (Luke 14:28–30), or a merchant (Matthew 13:45–46) – Jesus turns what they do into pictures of the kingdom of God. It's hard to resist the thought that this is part of the message: our work can picture the kingdom of God for us; indeed, we can work at it as members of the kingdom of God.

Paul says it all to the Colossians: 'Whatever you do, whether in word or deed, do it all in the name of the Lord Jesus, giving thanks to God the Father through him' (Colossians 3:17).

Questions

1. What about missionary societies? Would Paul approve of them, or not? And what about paid ministers? What would he say?
2. Can all work glorify God? Are there some jobs which Christians shouldn't do? Which? Why?
3. When should we resist appeals for help? How should we do it? This is a tricky question. Be very practical here and share examples and stories if you can.

2 Thessalonians 3:13–18

Living in peace with each other

Paul gives a fourth reason for work, as he winds his letter up with final instructions and loving greetings.

Verse 13 actually begins with a 'but', not an 'and'. A closer translation would be, 'But as for you, brothers and sisters, don't lose heart in doing what is right and good.' Paul has just been addressing the 'disorderly', the work-refusers, in verse 12. So these 'brothers and sisters' must be the rest of the church, on whom the work-refusers have been dependent.

Paul has just told these folk to be a bit tough-minded – don't give in to these requests, insist on the 'no work, no food' principle (verse 10). So now he redresses the balance a bit. He doesn't want them to stop giving altogether. On the contrary. The basic principle is to 'do what is right and good', which might mean giving to one person and refusing to give to another. So here is Paul's fourth reason for work.

We must work, so that we have something with which to do good (verse 13)

Jesus makes this point, in his parable of the unjust steward (Luke 16:1–13). Money is dreadful stuff, he says; it corrupts and demands worship and produces unrighteousness; but it can be used for the kingdom of God, if we handle it 'faithfully'.

And Paul makes this point too, very dramatically, in Ephesians 4:28. 'Thieves must give up stealing', he says. Rather, 'let them labour and work honestly with their own hands, so as to have something to share with the needy' (New Revised Standard Version). This balances up Paul's second reason for work – that we do it in order to feed ourselves. If this is the main reason, then work is a self-centred thing. But no! says Paul. In contrast to thieves who grab for themselves, he wants us to be workers who earn for others.

This involves a dramatic new perspective on that monthly payslip. For whom have you earned that money? You now have something with which to do good. Don't 'lose heart' – don't let the world tell you it's yours to spend how you like. What a lie! That's theft.

There is a very sharp difference between the Christian approach to work and money, and the non-Christian one. This explains the rather fierce-sounding verse 14, which actually looks back over the whole letter, and not just this last section. There can be no compromise between the two approaches. So if some insist that the Day of the Lord is past, and there is no future coming of the Lord, or if some withdraw from the world and refuse to work, making themselves dependent on hand-outs, then they are absolutely wrong, says Paul, and you can't 'associate' with such people.

This does not mean that we can't meet or speak with them. 'Associate' here means 'team up with', 'make common cause with'. It's the same word as Paul uses in

189

1 Corinthians 5:9, 11, where he tells the Corinthians that they cannot 'associate' with a brother or sister who is known as 'sexually immoral or greedy, an idolater or a slanderer, a drunkard or a swindler. With such a man do not even eat' (5:11). To eat with them would be to express fellowship with an absolutely wrong lifestyle. Paul has in mind people who are openly committed to these things, and see nothing wrong with them as Christians.

Paul clearly believed that sometimes it is right to withdraw fellowship from someone, 'in order that he may feel ashamed'. But he is quick to add the comment, 'Yet do not regard him as an enemy, but warn him as a brother.' Withdrawing fellowship doesn't mean breaking contact, nor does it mean denying brotherhood.

Paul knows well that there are people in the church in Thessalonica who will dispute his letter. They may come round to his viewpoint, or they may not. Either way, things are going to be tricky and tense in the church, especially if it is decided to take some disciplinary action. So his final prayer (verse 16) is very apt: 'Now may the Lord of peace himself give you peace at all times and in every way. The Lord be with all of you' – including the 'disorderly'. He longs to see the church living in the peace which the Lord alone can give. But they cannot have the Lord's peace except on the basis of the Lord's truth – and he is coming again, and he does command us to work.

Paul signs off, in his own handwriting (verse 17). His normal practice was to dictate his letters to a secretary (see *e.g.* Romans 16:22), but clearly he has decided, because of the danger of false letters (2:2), to add an authenticating signature to his letters from now on. We see the same at the end of 1 Corinthians (16:21), Galatians (6:11), Colossians (4:18) and Philemon (19). But he didn't always remember to do this.

His final greeting, which is also a prayer, commits his beloved Thessalonians to the grace of the Lord Jesus Christ, who alone can strengthen and deliver them in all the pressures they face (2:16–17).

Questions

1. Do you think that there is enough teaching in your church on the use of money? What are the main points that you would put into a teaching session on this?
2. Can you think of an example of the kind of church discipline that Paul has in mind here (verses 14–16)? Or of an application of 'church discipline' which runs against what Paul has in mind?
3. Think back over the whole of 2 Thessalonians. Write a letter to an imaginary aunt (or a real missionary friend) summarizing what God has taught you through it.

For further reading

F. F. Bruce, *1 and 2 Thessalonians*, Word Biblical Commentary (Word, 1982)

Mark Greene, *Thank God it's Monday* (Scripture Union, 1997)

John Stott, *The Message of Thessalonians*, The Bible Speaks Today (IVP, 1991)

Stephen Travis, *Christ and the Judgment of God: Divine Retribution in the New Testament* (Marshall Pickering, 1986)

Stephen Travis, *I Believe in the Second Coming of Jesus* (Hodder and Stoughton, 1982)